To Janet

with best

John Coue

26th September 1991

Your Problem Dog

Your Problem Dog

JOHN CREE

PELHAM BOOKS

PELHAM BOOKS

Published by the Penguin Group
27 Wrights Lane, London W8 5TZ, England
Viking Penguin, a division of Penguin Books USA Inc
375 Hudson Street, New York, NY 10014, USA
Penguin Books Australia Ltd, Ringwood, Victoria, Australia
Penguin Books Canada Ltd, 2801 John Street, Markham, Ontario, Canada L3R 1B4
Penguin Books (NZ) Ltd, 182–190 Wairau Road, Auckland 10, New Zealand

Penguin Books Ltd, Registered Offices: Harmondsworth, Middlesex, England

First Published 1991
10 9 8 7 6 5 4 3 2 1

Printed in England by Clays Ltd, St Ives
Typeset in 10/12½ pt Photina

A CIP catalogue record for this book is available from the British Library.

ISBN 0 7207 1976 3

To my grandchildren –

STEPHEN and ELAINE BALL

GORDON and SHEENA RAE

The future of our canine companions will become
the responsibility of their generation.

Contents

Problem References

Acknowledgements

The knowledge expressed in this book is like that of many others, it has been gathered from an indeterminable variety of sources over a great number of years. However, there must be at least one particular source of inspiration which has created a foundation for the thinking process which has resulted in the approach and techniques which become apparent in this publication.

That particular inspiration is a book titled *Dog Training – A Manual* by Colonel Konrad Most. It was given to me as a Christmas present in 1958 and became an important guide for future development.

The photographs were taken principally with the cooperation of Fiona and Mike McFadyen and Frances Ball, and I thank them for their assistance.

As with my previous books, Irene, my wife, has had to play a principal role in reviewing the manuscript, typing and altering as necessary to ensure that the end product becomes a fitting addition to my earlier publications.

Introduction

Dogs are part of our community and one way or another they affect the lives of all of us. Their presence gives us companionship and relaxation; they give us pleasure, enjoyment and a loyalty which we gratefully accept. However, they are a responsibility and, like any other responsibility in our lives, dogs require consideration. We must learn about their needs, their wants and their ways. We can go wrong, we can fail to appreciate the needs of our canine companions and we can fail to take into account the effect that a dog's presence has on other members of the community.

Other dog owners, the elderly, children, tradesmen and the like are all affected by the presence of our dogs. It is excellent if that presence is appreciated and accepted with pleasure, but in many cases it is not.

Because of lack of knowledge, understanding, or a failure to appreciate the effect of our actions, canine behaviour is not always equivalent to our expectations or requirements. Canine behaviour situations can cause unpleasantness or embarrassment both in the home and within the community. Situations can become intolerable and the dog has to go, either to a new home or to be permanently put to sleep. With many intolerable situations the owner puts up with it and accepts his cross to bear.

We speak of canine behaviour problems, but in fact, to the dog, his behaviour is not a problem. He is doing what nature intended and he never considers his behaviour to be anti-social. His behaviour may make life unpleasant for us and we may make life unpleasant for him but something must be done to create a more acceptable behaviour pattern.

The problems all start with ourselves as dog owners and there are several questions we must ask ourselves:

- Did we purchase the most suitable type of dog for our environment?
- Do we have a suitable environment for any type of dog?
- Did we obtain a puppy or an older dog with unsociable habits?
- Did we obtain a dog for the right reasons?
- Did we consider his previous environment and behavioural tendencies?
- Have we given him a suitable basic training?
- Do we really appreciate his needs?
- Do we have him understanding our needs?

Honest answers to these questions can help us understand the reasons why your canine companion has become *your problem dog.*

Our canine problems are really a result of our own shortcomings and when looking at a problem we must look first at ourselves. We may have to change our thinking, our actions or our attitudes to achieve a satisfactory solution to the problem. A change must come from within if we wish to alter a dog's behaviour pattern.

Although canine psychology is a specialised subject, a layman's appreciation of its principles is a great advantage in understanding and curing a behaviour problem. A knowledge and the application of basic control training are other ingredients which help us to achieve a more pleasurable canine companionship. The initial chapters in this book give an introduction to both canine psychology and basic control requirements to ensure that the reader has a foundation on which to establish the changes which are necessary to overcome any behaviour problems.

The problems one normally encounters are many and varied. One of the principal difficulties is that of analysing the causes of the various troublesome situations. With each problem listed in this book, probable causes will be discussed along with suggested methods of achieving satisfactory behaviour in the future.

There can be a variety of remedies for a single problem and there are single remedies which can be used to counter a variety of problems. However, there are remedies which require the involvement of an expert where his ability and his experience are of paramount importance. These specified remedies do not come within the scope of this book as it would be very unwise for an inexperienced person to use such methods.

The remedies discussed should lie within the ability of the average dog owner. It is important that the information up to and including Chapter Four be fully studied, understood and revised from time to time. The simple but basic training described in Chapter Two should be successfully accomplished before tackling the remedies for any of the problems discussed in the remainder of the text.

For simplicity throughout this book the use of the male gender will apply to both sexes unless specifically detailed. The use of the word 'owner' will also be used throughout to mean the person in control of the dog during behaviour or training situations.

CHAPTER ONE

Understanding Your Dog

Although the subject of this chapter is understanding dogs, consideration must also be given to understanding the people who are involved with dogs. Canine behaviour is generally related to the person in control most of the time. A dog is likely to act or react in a particular way with one member of the family but can behave in a completely different manner with some other person.

A dog will react to a show of strength in the human personality. Indecisiveness or inconsistency are probably high on the list of human failings which result in uncontrolled canine situations. Brutish or uncompromising attitudes from a human being can be equally responsible for unsatisfactory canine responses. Every person involved with a dog must, therefore, consider his own outlook when assessing the actions and reactions of our canine friends.

The personal approach must always be considered when applying the various principles being discussed throughout this book.

CANINE LOGIC

The appreciation of canine logic is the first step towards understanding the causes of behaviour problems and this logic is best described as –

A DOG WILL ALWAYS DO WHAT HE CONSIDERS TO BE IN HIS BEST INTEREST AT THAT PARTICULAR MOMENT IN TIME.

Although this logic may also be apportioned to human beings, there are significant differences between the interpretations relating to dogs and humans. There are many factors which control the actions or reactions of a human being, such as

- Sense of responsibility
- Duty towards others
- Fairness with others
- Community laws and regulations.

These are only a selection of the factors which affect the logical decisions which are made by man.

It is safe to assume that a dog is not inhibited by any such restrictions or responsibilities. It can be said that canine loyalty and affection influence behaviour patterns, and there may be a certain amount of truth in this way of thinking, but false confidence can be gained by thinking that a dog will react to a person's wishes solely out of loyalty or affection, which must first be earned. People must understand that canine logic is based on the instincts of survival and includes the dog's interpretation of how human behaviour is likely to affect him at any particular time.

CANINE v HUMAN APPRECIATION

A dog's level of understanding does not include blame or punishment, nor does it include praise or reward. Man, on the other hand, has rather fixed interpretations of the meaning of these expressions that are best explained by extracts from the *Oxford Dictionary* –

BLAME   – To find fault with
PUNISHMENT   – Penalty inflicted on offender
PRAISE   – To express warm approbation (approval) of
REWARD   – Recompense for service or merit.

If our interpretation of canine logic is to be accepted a dog cannot be *blamed* or judged to be at fault for any action which is considered to be undesirable by the owner or members of the community. To blame the dog would be to divert the responsibility from the true source and, as the dog cannot be blamed, there is no place for the application of punishment at any time. With the use of *punishment* as an expression when describing a human reaction to canine behaviour there is a great danger that the meaning and, therefore, the resulting action, can be incorrectly applied.

Because of the fixed impressions within the human mind neither blame nor punishment should be directed against a dog and must be strongly discouraged with owners or others involved in assessing canine behaviour. The alternatives will be discussed shortly.

Although a dog does not understand the expressions *praise* or *reward* as such, the human application does fall into line with the reactions which are desirable from a dog. Therefore, the use of these expressions is quite acceptable so long as there is a full understanding of their application and the relationship to the alternative expression.

Canine understanding, however, is based on what is pleasant or unpleasant at a particular time. By applying these types of reaction with the appropriate timing much can be achieved to prevent or correct undesirable canine behaviour. A *pleasant* human reaction at the correct time will help to induce the desired canine response and an *unpleasant* human reaction can arrest an unacceptable canine activity.

The timing of those pleasant or unpleasant human reactions is of vital importance and the question now is: What is the correct timing? It is a very short space of time that can best be described as starting from the ideal and continuing to the latest moment of human reaction. In most cases two or three seconds of time can be considered to be too long and can be ineffective.

The time lapse starts when the dog is thinking of acting in a particular manner and this is the *ideal* time. The period finishes as the dog is completing the particular action and this is the *latest* time.

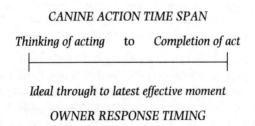

CANINE ACTION TIME SPAN

Thinking of acting   to   *Completion of act*

Ideal through to latest effective moment

OWNER RESPONSE TIMING

The effectiveness of human reaction can also be said to be in relation to the timing: the most effective reaction being obtained during the canine thinking period. If an owner is sufficiently observant he can recognise when his dog is thinking of acting in a particular manner. In fact, past experience should warn an owner of these occasions. Whilst out for a walk with a dog the sight of another dog relatively close may cause an aggressive reaction. If the owner sees the other dog first he can observe his dog's reaction to the other dog's presence before his creates an aggressive situation. This knowledge can give an owner time to take preventive action and divert his dog's attention before he has the opportunity to show the unpleasant side of his nature. Strong and urgent diverting action on the owner's part whilst the dog is thinking of acting, which is then repeated on subsequent occasions, will have the dog watching for his owner's reaction. This will take his attention away from the other dog and will be much more effective than if the owner reacted after the event.

Another example is teaching a puppy to retrieve. The first step is to teach the puppy to pick up an article when required. Puppies, particularly those with a plentiful supply of toys at home, will pick up articles of their own choice at will. When a puppy notices an article of interest that is not forbidden and is thinking of picking it up, a few words of gentle encouragement from the owner can let him know that he is pleased with his thoughts and that he can proceed. If this is repeated on a number of occasions when they arise, an opportunity can be taken to kick some suitable article to draw the puppy's attention to it. As soon as this happens the tone of encouragement previously employed can be used to help the puppy to pick up the article that the owner wants him to carry.

These are just a few examples of observation, timing and human actions – pleasant or unpleasant – which are used to create the desired canine reaction.

A pleasant reaction must always follow the effectiveness of an unpleasant action or reaction. The effectiveness of an unpleasant human reaction is indicated by the fact that the dog has been prevented from carrying out or continuing with undesirable behaviour. In either case the dog is acting in a desirable manner. The unpleasantness creates the change and the pleasant human reaction that follows acknowledges that the dog is acting in a desirable manner.

The degree and nature of the unpleasantness is determined by the situation. A sharp single word such as NO or a hard stamp of the owner's foot on the ground to gain attention may be sufficient to achieve the desired result. On the other hand, a hefty tug on the lead along with the blast of a few choice words may be necessary to regain a controlled situation. Whatever the action, it must not be carried out with malice, anger or brutality and should be followed immediately with praise and a reward which, of course, is a pleasant reaction.

Praise in itself is a reward and must be given with feeling. The praise may be in the nature of a few words, such as 'that's a good boy' said with appropriate feeling, or it may just be a gentle fondling of the dog. Any other form of reward should be supplementary to praise and not instead of it. A titbit or fun with a toy can be considered a reward and supplementary to praise.

COMMUNICATING WITH A DOG

A dog must be able to understand requirements before he can be expected to react to them. These requirements may be projected by sound, sight or feel or by any combination of the three. When a dog has translated these requirements he will act in response to canine logic.

Requirements by sound generally mean verbal instructions, but a clap of the hands, a whistle or some unintelligible noise from the vocal chords can be applied as a means of communication.

There is a language barrier between man and dog and it should, therefore, be recognised that a dog does not learn from words but from actions. The meaning of a word or noise becomes synonymous with the appropriate action.

Sign language and physical assistance can initially achieve desired results where words of instruction will fail to have any effect. If a dog is being trained to sit when instructed it is quite useless to give the verbal instruction to sit if he has not been introduced to the meaning of the word. However, a sit position can be enticed or physically induced by the owner's actions. When these actions become meaningful to the dog verbal instructions will then begin to have some meaning.

A sound or action from an owner will tell a dog something. However, he can only react to the owner's wishes if these factors have been correctly translated and to translate dependably there must be consistency in the messages which are being sent from owner to dog. Owner inconsistency can only cause canine confusion.

CANINE ATTENTIVENESS AND CONFLICTS OF INTEREST

Without the dog's attention the owner has no control. If there is nothing occupying a dog's mind his attention will be easily attained, particularly if he expects a follow-up action to be pleasant. However, if there is a strong conflict of interest – the dog is distracted by something and the owner requires his attention – a real problem has developed. The ease or difficulty in gaining a dog's attention is dependent on the degree of conflict and the dog's assessment of the value of cooperation at that moment in time.

The ability to gain a dog's attention at any particular time is very important to an owner. The ability to recognise that the conflict of interest is too great to achieve success under the prevailing conditions is also important to an owner so that he may create conditions which will bring success.

The foundation of good control and of a sound response is based on an owner's ability to gain a dog's attention, to retain it and then to make use of it in a manner which leads the dog to believe it is in his own best interest to comply with the situation the owner has created.

Distance between dog and owner can have a dramatic effect on a dog's response and this can vary from one dog to another. A great distance between dog and owner can give the dog the feeling of independence: he is out of reach and is not required to react favourably towards his owner. On the other hand, the dog may become worried as he realises that such a distance separates him from his master and this can induce a very favourable reaction.

These effective distances can vary considerably from dog to dog. The realisation that there are ten yards between one dog and his owner can induce a positive response one way or another from the dog, but with a different dog it may require fifty to one hundred yards of separation to create the same response. This varying in distance can cause the apparent inconsistencies which many owners experience with their dogs.

It is important to recognise that *success breeds success* but *failure encourages confusion*. With this in mind owners should appreciate the need to *create* success out of possible failure situations.

CONTROL EQUIPMENT AND ADDITIONAL TRAINING AIDS FOR IMPROVING BEHAVIOUR

The choice and variety of equipment and the numerous training aids can play a significant part in an owner's ability to achieve success with his dog in training. Although collars and leads are the principal pieces of equipment there are other items which must be given consideration. They are grouped as:

CONTROL EQUIPMENT
1. Various types of collar
2. Suitable leads
3. Lines of various lengths

ADDITIONAL TRAINING AIDS
1. Titbits
2. Other attention-getting aids.

CONTROL EQUIPMENT

The principles and application of control equipment should be understood by the owner to obtain the greatest value out of the chosen items. The various combinations of equipment utilised have three basic functions:

1. As the principal controlling aid for training – apart from giving the owner confidence that he can handle the situation and that the application of these items helps to convince the dog that it is in his best interest to cooperate.
2. As an effective measure of restraint when situations develop which are beyond the control of the owner and the dog.
3. As a controlling factor to be utilised when the owner is not in a position to give the dog his full attention.

Although the three basic functions have just been given, the choice of equipment is generally governed by the requirements of control for training.

Collars

The choice of collar can play a significant part in the owner's ability to control his dog, although generally speaking it is the application of both collar and lead or line which controls the effectiveness of an owner's actions.

Unless in the hands of an expert, the conventional *buckle* type of collar has little effect on an owner's ability to control his dog and is not generally recommended.

Check collars come in a variety of styles with the most commonly used being known as the *check chain*. The problem with the metal linked chain type is its ability to cut away at the hairs around the dog's neck every time tension is applied; the small link chains do most damage. Check collars are also made of leather, flat or round, nylon webbing or rope and often it is just a matter of choice which is preferred.

These check collars should be chosen to suit the size of the dog and ideally should just be able to slip over the dog's head with little to spare. An overlong check collar round a dog's neck may affect an owner's application of collar and lead; it can also fall off and get lost or it can get caught up with something which could create a dangerous situation.

With a properly fitting check collar a short but sharp jerk on the lead should gain the dog's attention to terminate an uncontrolled situation or in preparation for a more attentive and constructive period. It is important that this type of collar is put over the dog's head in the correct manner. With the dog at the handler's left side the collar is worn in such a manner that it will automatically slacken off when any tension is released.

The *combi-collar* is an excellent alternative to the check collar. This style has a short chain loop which is attached to a webbing band which is adjustable. The collar is easily adjusted to slip neatly over the dog's head and in action it has a limited amount of slip. It is a convenient and effective collar for training and for general use.

Another concept which has been introduced by Dr Roger Mugford for canine control is the *halti*. This is a form of head harness instead of a collar, and control is applied with the lead attached to a ring under the dog's lower jaw. It is a most effective form of control and is particularly useful for owners who find it difficult to control their dogs.

Leads

A good strong lead with a dependable clip attachment is essential. The standard length of four to five feet is ideal for training and normal handling practices. Shorter leads do not give the handler room to manoeuvre for prevention or corrective action and longer leads can become difficult to handle.

Although a good quality leather lead is ideal, the use of soft nylon or cotton webbing can be equally suitable. Chain leads are very hard on the hands of an owner and make it difficult for him to apply proper control techniques; chain leads should, therefore, be avoided.

Flexi-leads which automatically retract have a length of up to twenty-five feet and can be of value in training for canine control. The flexi-lead can be locked, if desired, at any length to suit the situation or it can be allowed to run out or in at will. This type of lead is not easily handled for training in loose lead walking and it is not recommended for this purpose. It can be utilised for testing the effect of loose lead walking training where complete freedom is given to the flexi movement. The dog knows he is attached, but the owner also knows that movement and verbal actions are required on his part to control the situation, rather than tugs on the lead.

The flexi-lead, however, has greater uses when applied instead of lines of various lengths and this will be discussed in the next section.

Lines

With many dogs a dragging line is an inhibiting factor and great use can be made of this means of control in training. Although lines can be of any length there are certain lengths which are ideally suited to particular purposes or to counter certain canine reactions.

The most suitable lines are made of nylon cord and of a size which has a listed breaking strain of approximately 700 lb (318 kg). Lengths or reels of this cord can be purchased from ironmongers, D.I.Y. stores and some sports shops. On these lines it is advisable to attach a trigger clip of the type that is used on the end of standard leads. When required, a holding loop can be tied on the other end of the line.

Suitable lines and applications using this approach are as follows:

1. A thirty foot line with a trigger clip at one end and a loop at the other can be used as a dragging line for dogs which will not come back when called.

2.a. A six foot line with a trigger clip at one end can be utilised instead of the thirty foot line or to replace it before giving the dog greater freedom.

b. This line can also be used indoors where there are no knots or attachments which can catch under doors, etc.

3. A flexi-lead can be used for getting attention and countering recall behaviour problems to give some distance between dog and owner. The flexi-lead would be utilised in the same way as the lead for attention getting and the flexi-lead will automatically retract as the dog returns. However, the owner does not have quite the same freedom to use both hands for encouragement or to achieve a balanced welcome.

Additional Training Aids

Additional aids can be very useful in achieving an owner's objective. These aids should never replace praise or a pleasant owner disposition. They should, in actual fact, be supplementary.

The philosophy of these training aids is based on the pleasant handler response as described under the heading Canine Logic on pages 15 and 16. With the understanding attained from the explanation regarding pleasant reactions these aids will now be termed *rewards*.

The timing of rewards is very critical and has already been described as owner response timing on pages 17 and 18. These rewards can be placed into two separate categories:

1. Titbits
2. Play toys.

The use of titbits can be very effective but some thought should be given to the type of food which is going to be used for a particular dog. Although some dogs will react to almost any kind of titbit, the type which generates the greatest enthusiasm should be used. Many dogs will react reasonably well to a dog biscuit but will show real enthusiasm when cooked and dried liver cubes are presented. Others will do almost anything for a piece of cheese and there are, of course, some very appetising packaged titbits. Some owners have used small cat titbits to great effect.

Presentation of titbits is as important as the tasty morsels themselves. It should be recognised that dogs cannot see titbits from a distance, but their presentation in a plastic bag or some obvious container can be very effective. A dog can see a plastic bag and can also hear it rustle. The noise of titbits rattling in a container also can be very effective and, with the knowledge that titbits are there for the taking, can be sufficient to bring a dog back when no amount of calling will have any effect.

The actual presentation of the titbits can affect results and it is now found to be preferable to have the dog come in close enough to take the titbit from the owner rather than for the owner to give the dog the titbit. The owner should hold the bag of titbits close to his body (at the dog's nose level if possible) after letting the dog see that they are available. The owner takes a titbit into his clenched hand with palm facing outwards. When the dog comes in and sniffs at the hand, or bag if both hands are together, he opens the hand and lets the dog take his reward.

The clenched hand principle can be utilised at other times, such as with loose lead walking, but the positioning of the hand alters to suit the occasion.

Play toys can also be used instead of titbits but to give the dog full benefit of fun and games with them as a reward generally results in a loss of control and, in the early stages of behaviour improvement training, it is important that control is maintained. Play toys can be successfully used on a number of occasions but owners must be selective in their choice of application.

CHAPTER TWO

Elementary Control

A very high proportion of canine behaviour problems are due to the owner's inability to obtain or keep his dog's attention when it is required. Without this ability to attract and maintain attentive contact little, if anything, can ever be achieved.

If an owner wants his dog to come back when called he must gain the dog's attention first. If the dog ignores the call of his name or some other approach to attention getting there is little hope of getting him to come back at that moment. If he is chewing his owner's slipper his attention must be diverted if there is to be a chance of getting him to leave the slipper alone.

It will therefore be appreciated that the foundation of any form of canine control is based on the ability to gain a dog's attentiveness under situations where there are conflicts of interest as described in the previous chapter.

An attention-getting routine is described in this chapter along with the training required to have the dog sit and stay sitting in the vicinity of the owner. This pattern of elementary control is the foundation required for curing so many behaviour problems. Subsequent training routines to suit individual problems will be described in the appropriate places.

Any training or conditioning routine should be taken in stages if satisfactory progress is to be made. It is important that each stage in the learning process be achieved before progressing to the next.

BASIC CONTROL TRAINING ROUTINE

This routine has two principal objectives and these objectives are achieved progressively through a sequence of interlinked stages. These stages are called *targets* and each target is a link in the training process or an objective in itself.

The targets have been devised to help the owner assess the levels of progress. It is very important not to try to progress beyond the dog's stage of competence, but to work for and consolidate at each target level.

The principal objectives are to

- gain and keep the dog's attention for a short period of time.
- have the dog sit and stay sitting for a short period of time whilst in the vicinity of the owner.

The general approach to these objectives is to ensure that the dog will give his owner full attention when it is required and will then respond to any reasonable follow-up activity.

To give the dog some purpose for giving his attention to his owner and also for the follow-up activity, the dog must be prepared to watch and follow his owner's every movement. The owner's movement will develop so that it will be alternating at times between backward and forward. During this development the dog will be expected to sit at the owner's side on completion of a forward movement and sit in front of the owner on completion of a backward movement. The dog also remains sitting as the owner walks round him within a lead's length.

In achieving these objectives the foundation has been laid for a more controlled canine companion and a much more stable relationship between dog and owner.

FIRST TARGET

The dog should respond to the call of his name and move on a loose lead towards his owner as he is moving backwards and drawing his dog towards him. If possible this should be carried out with minor or no distractions to the dog and just for a few seconds.

TRAINING ROUTINE

With the dog on the lead the action to be applied is that of the owner making a smart backward movement, if necessary to be accompanied by a sharp jerk on the lead and the use of the dog's name to obtain his immediate attention. A continuation of this backward movement for a few seconds will ensure that the dog's attention is maintained. If canine attention deviates from the owner due to some distraction, changing direction to the left or right and away from the distraction will probably be necessary to regain full attention.

Distractions can be varied in type but, in the open, distractions will come and go, and an attractively scented lamppost is all that is required to divert the attention of some dogs. Canine boredom in itself can be turned to advantage for the attention-getting routine.

The use and timing of the dog's name is very important. The use of the dog's name must be developed as the principal means of gaining the dog's attention.

The name should be used with urgency but not with harshness. Although great volume is not required there should be sufficient penetration to be effective. The use of the name is applied *immediately* prior to the backward movement and accompanied by a jerk on the lead if it is required. There should be no time lag between calling the name and the physical movement.

The dog's attention is maintained at this stage by a continual use of the voice and with phrases encouraging him to follow the owner. A phrase such as 'Come on son, hurry up' repeated or changed as necessary should be sufficient. The handling of the lead, hand and arm actions and body posture are equally important features for maintaining canine attention.

It is preferable to have the loop at the end of the lead over the thumb of the right hand, to be held when necessary in the clenched hand. When the owner is moving backwards and the dog is expected to follow attentively and with enthusiasm, hands and lead should be kept low with the lead/collar attachment below the dog's lower jaw. With palms of hands facing upwards the handler should be using encouraging movements with fingers and arms. If possible the hands should be held level with the dog's eyes although it is appreciated that this is not practical with small dogs.

The dog is encouraged to move faster than the owner so that the dog will finish close to the owner and facing him. In achieving this situation the lead must be kept loose but should be gradually taken in by both left and right hands in a manner which will allow the owner to drop the lead, except for the loop on the right thumb when alternative action is required. This alternative action can counter canine distraction during backward movement.

SECOND TARGET

With strong distractions being applied the dog should respond to the call of his name and move on a loose lead towards the owner as the latter is moving backwards and drawing his dog with him. His attention should be gained for a five to ten second period.

TRAINING ROUTINE

This activity repeats the first target but with the application of some stronger distractions. The attraction between two dogs can be friendly or aggressively based and it is best to graduate from friendly-based situations so that the owner can assess his ability to handle other situations.

The owner, with the dog on the lead, can start from some ten to fifteen paces from the distraction and walk directly towards it. Any attempt by the dog to move ahead of the owner or to pull on the lead must immediately be countered by backward movement as described in the training routine relating to the first target. With very strong distractions firm handling is required and immediate praise should be given when the dog cooperates enthusiastically. Remember that canine enthusiasm can be a reaction to human enthusiasm.

THIRD TARGET

After moving backwards with the dog on the lead the owner should now be able to change direction by moving forward so that the dog must turn and fall in at the owner's left side for a few paces. Alternating owner movement backward then forward with varying distractions should be attained for a period of up to thirty seconds.

TRAINING ROUTINE

This stage brings in the first step in training for loose lead walking.

Forward movement after moving away from a distraction gives the dog the opportunity to reactivate his interest in the distraction. Any return of this interest must be controlled by another change to backward movement.

When alternating between backward and forward movements the backward movement should take in at least six paces but more may be required to ensure that attention is maintained. The amount of forward movement is controlled by the dog's ability to maintain an attentive position with his head approximately in line with the owner's left leg. On completion of this stage, half a minute of full attention should be attainable without the dog's attention wandering away from his owner at any time.

Changing from backward to forward movement can be achieved by the owner moving to the dog's right side so that the dog turns towards the owner's left side as they are passing each other. The left arm moves out to the side so that the section of the lead slipping through the left hand helps to guide the dog.

As soon as both dog and owner are moving forward in the same direction the pattern of lead control is again important. With the loop at the end of the lead still over the right thumb the lead can be gathered in the right hand so that the surplus is at the owner's right side and does not become a hindrance.

With both arms extended downwards and relaxed, a hand should be in front of each leg. There should be approximately six to eight inches of lead between the left and right hands and a minimum of lead between the dog's collar and the left hand. However, the lead between dog and owner should not be tight. The left hand can hold the lead, serve as a guide for the lead or be used freely for encouragement as and how the circumstances demand.

Occasionally forward movement can be punctuated by a halt every single or double step. The dog is not being asked to sit during these punctuated stops but should take the steps with the owner and stand still with every momentary stop. Any failure to do so will require a smart backward movement and this is to be continued until the dog reacts correctly to the owner's movements. Distance from a distraction has a great deal of effect. The closer the dog is to the distraction the greater the canine concentration required to maintain his position at the owner's left side.

Note: Time can be taken to work on and consolidate at this stage, and at the same time the sitting element of training can be introduced via the fourth target.

FOURTH TARGET

The dog should be prepared to stay sitting when put into that position by the owner. The owner can stand straddled over the dog while both are facing in the same direction to ensure that the dog does not move. (With small dogs it may be more convenient for the owner to kneel with the dog positioned between his knees.)

TRAINING ROUTINE

The approach to this target is to have the dog sit promptly and attentively at the owner's left side before the latter stands straddled over him. The owner should start with the dog on the lead and standing at his left side.

The owner takes the lead in his right hand as close to the dog's collar as possible and at the same time puts his left hand at the left side of the dog's croup, pushing his rear end down and to the right as the other hand pulls on the lead. This double action to be carried out with coordination and purpose.

As this function is being carried out the owner should talk attentively to his dog and, as he is going into the sit position, give a positive sit instruction.

Immediately the dog is in the sit position the owner should stand straddled over the dog with his hands stroking the dog's neck to give him reassurance and also to be ready to prevent the dog from changing his position, either to stand up or to lie down. The dog can be praised for staying in that position as long as the owner is able to prevent movement.

Initially a five second stay in this position is quite sufficient before giving the dog freedom. The giving of freedom to break the stay position should be just as positive as the instruction to sit. At no time should the dog move without full and enthusiastic permission from the owner.

FIFTH TARGET

The dog should be able to stay in the sit position for at least ten seconds while the owner stands in front of him, or on occasion walks round him at the end of a loose lead. At no time should the dog move from the sit position until instructed.

TRAINING ROUTINE

Before progressing from the straddled position the owner should ensure that his dog will accept gentle to enthusiastic praise without moving while he is in a position to prevent such movement if it becomes necessary. Progress can be made when the dog accepts this praise without showing any intention of movement.

With the lead in his hand the owner can then break contact with the dog by taking half a step backwards and keeping his feet well apart so that he is still in a position to anticipate canine movement and act accordingly. During the training for this target the lead must be kept loose as the owner starts to move round the dog with the use of gentle praise and firm but quiet instructions to stay. Any canine movement must still be anticipated and caught before any initial movement results in a complete change in position, such as standing or lying down.

The owner should eventually be able to stand still in front of the dog at the end of a loose lead for a full ten seconds without any indication of canine movement.

Note: The attention-getting and sit objectives can now be combined for the remainder of the training routines.

SIXTH TARGET

While he remains at the owner's left side the dog should be prepared to sit as soon as he is given the instruction. This should be carried out without any physical assistance.

TRAINING ROUTINE

This is principally a stage which confirms the effect of positive sit training for the earlier targets. The dog should now be sitting immediately on the verbal instruction from the owner. The assistance of visual signals such as body, arm or hand movements – or the use of titbits to induce the appropriate action – is quite permissible and is encouraged to ensure an immediate response. A response must be attained on the first instruction although this instruction should be preceded by the use of the dog's name as an attention getter.

SEVENTH TARGET

When the owner halts on completion of a forward movement the dog should be prepared to sit smartly at the owner's left side.

TRAINING ROUTINE

The third target being accomplished with enthusiasm and satisfaction now leads on to a controlled finish – having the dog sit nicely at the owner's left side when he halts.

The details for achieving this sit should already be accomplished quite independently under training for the fourth, fifth and sixth targets. Initially it may be necessary for the owner to give physical assistance along with the instruction to sit to ensure that the dog responds immediately when the owner halts. This is best performed by using the following approach: within a step of halting the owner moves his right hand over to hold the lead as close to the collar as is practical. This controls the movement of the dog's forequarters as the owner halts and releases the left hand to push in at the left side of the dog's croup to ensure a quick and controlled sit. The timing of a verbal instruction to sit will soon ensure that the dog responds without physical assistance.

As soon as the dog sits, gentle praise should be applied while the dog is made to hold the sit position for some five seconds. Abundant praise can then be given when the dog is released from the finished sit position.

EIGHTH AND FINAL TARGET

When the owner halts on completion of the backward movement he

should be able to have his dog sit in front of and facing him, reasonably close to his body and with an attentive outlook.

TRAINING ROUTINE

As the dog has already been trained to sit at the owner's left side and to do so without physical assistance, there should not be any difficulty in getting him to sit in front. Although physical handling can be applied to achieve the objective, inducements will produce a much more attentive frame of mind.

Initially, the dog sits whilst on the lead at the owner's left side, then the owner moves round so that he is standing close and in front of the dog. The owner gives the dog a titbit or gains his attention with a toy, he then inches backwards about half to one step and draws the dog back with him using verbal and visual encouragement along with a titbit or some other inducement.

A short movement forward to maintain closeness to the owner does not allow the dog a real chance to stand up. The verbal instruction to sit and the visual aid with the inducement to draw the dog's head up should achieve the close sit position. Then reward as before.

When this short movement becomes easily accomplished the owner should move backwards a few paces with the dog following attentively, then halt to encourage the dog to sit close to and facing him. This procedure can then be developed into the full attention-getting routine.

Training, even elementary training, activates the mind. It makes the dog think and respond; it also makes owners think about their own ability to achieve some sort of cooperative reaction from their dogs. This is the first, but most important, step in preventing or correcting canine behaviour problems.

CHAPTER THREE

An Understanding of Behaviour Problems

To understand canine behaviour problems we should first try to appreciate the cause or causes of these problems. As stated in the first chapter the dog never considers that his actions are anti-social. He does not consider that he is being disobedient nor does he judge his actions to be the cause of some displeasure to his owner or the neighbourhood. He is only doing what he considers to be in his best interests at that particular time.

Canine behaviour problems are our problems and to change the pattern of a dog's behaviour to suit our needs requires the ability to analyse the situations in a manner which will highlight the probable causes. Some of the questions which should be considered are:

- Is the behaviour pattern inherent in that breed of dog?
- Is the problem evident through a particular strain within that breed?
- Is the present environment the cause of the problem?
- Has the environment of an earlier part of his life caused the problem?
- Are you or members of the family directly responsible for the undesirable canine actions?
- Is the behaviour pattern caused by a combination of the above?

It is sometimes difficult to analyse the true cause of a problem and often enough the true facts cannot be ascertained for various reasons. The dog's previous history may not be known, the problem may not be fully understood or the owner may not wish to divulge his own previous attitude or actions towards the dog.

These are factors which affect the ability of any behaviour specialist who is trying to solve the problem. They must also affect the reader of this book in trying to appreciate the reasons for particular examples of canine behaviour.

However, canine psychology is akin to canine medical care. The cause of the problem may not have to be understood to find the cure. The cause of some skin ailments in dogs is unknown to the practising vet – it could be one of a variety of causes – but he has a cure for the ailment. Unfortunately, the disorder may return at a later date because the origin has not been understood and averted.

Our own young German Shepherd Dog went down with haemorraghic gastroenteritis; we almost lost him but veterinary expertise and dedication saved his life. The vet did not know the actual cause of the ailment in this instance, but he cured the dog. It is the same with some behaviour problems, remedies can often be found and applied without knowledge of the cause. However, the vet and canine behaviourist have a far better chance of applying or recommending satisfactory remedial action if they can analyse the source of the problem.

In some cases the problem can be too deep-rooted to obtain a cure. A dog with a medical condition which has gone on too long or has caused irreversible damage may be beyond the scope of veterinary expertise. The same can happen with behaviour problems.

A dog with a deep-rooted behaviour problem may require intensive conditioning by an expert and a permanent change of environment to create a manageable situation. A suitable expert may not be available, the cost may be too high or the source of the problem may be an unsuitable environment. If any of these situations cannot be satisfactorily countered, the dog may experience an early termination of his life. It is such a pity that any dog's life should come to an early conclusion because of human inadequacies, but there are times when suitable alternatives are just not available.

SOURCE OF PROBLEMS

The earlier that undesirable behaviour is recognised the less chance there is of it becoming a real problem. Unfortunately many of these behaviour patterns grow out of amusing situations. An eight-week-old puppy who runs away is easily caught and it can be fun in this 'chase me – catch me' situation, but in a few weeks this puppy can run much faster and he learns to dodge and get into inaccessible places. Fun turns to human anger, human anger turns into puppy fear and a problem has been created.

A twelve-week-old puppy – be it a Jack Russell or a Rottweiler – just clear of inoculations is taken out for his first walk on the lead. He is small with little strength compared to an adult owner. He can pull on the lead with no discomfort to the owner, in fact it might be considered to be rather funny. The practice of pulling has started and the puppy grows into maturity without knowing anything different. The owner knows a big difference. The Jack Russell, although a small dog, has strength and power and can make daily walks unpleasant outings with his pulling and darting all over the place. The Rottweiler owner is in a different predicament with 132 lb (60 kg) or more of pure muscle straining at the end of the lead. Both owners have a problem which could have been avoided by simple conditioning to the lead before that first outing.

The sources of so many problems are as basic as the examples already given. It requires foresight and education to help dog owners appreciate the simple beginnings of significant problems.

All too often it is the dog who is dictating how and when things are done. He has become the leader instead of following the lead given by his owner. A dog wants to get up on the bed and enjoy the comfort and he is allowed to do so. He demands to be fed and is fed, he wants to be on the settee to curl up and be petted and he is not discouraged. Every little demand is met without question. However, there are times when little demands are not convenient. The dog comes in from a walk wet and dirty, then jumps up on the bed. He demands to be fed when visitors are being entertained or, while casting his coat, he jumps up on the settee between the owner and a visitor, leaving the loose hair on the visitor's suit.

All these little demands become habits and the dog considers each and every one to be his right. He can become upset and at times may turn nasty when he is refused one of the rights he has gained through custom and practice.

An act of canine behaviour once repeated is likely to become a habit – be it good or bad.

REMEDIAL ACTION

Many remedial actions to counter behaviour problems carry certain degrees of unpleasantness to the dog and corrective measures generally take time to establish the desired behaviour pattern.

There are actions which once applied are unlikely to require a repeat – once is sufficient. The effect of such actions is so strong and unpleasant that the dog will never consider behaving in such a manner again.

We would never consider deliberately shutting an estate car tail gate on a dog's ear, but once done by accident the dog will not forget to keep well clear of that tail gate for some considerable time – perhaps for ever. Put a sheep chaser into a pen with a ram or a ewe with a lamb to look after and the experience will be unforgettable. The dog will never go near sheep again. However, many people would refuse to put their dogs through such a harrowing experience, myself included.

Drastic action will normally have some side effect and great care must be taken before considering the use of instant cures. This does not mean that they should never be used; some are worthy of consideration but others should be avoided in favour of methods which take a little more time to establish the desired response.

The principles discussed in Chapter One along with the elementary control training in Chapter Two form the foundation for remedial action to counter behaviour problems.

CHAPTER FOUR

The Behaviour Problems

The variety of canine behaviour problems is never-ending and where problems are acknowledged by the dog owner there is generally more than one undesirable situation which is causing concern.

From a survey I have carried out on behaviour problems requiring my assistance, there can be anywhere between one and five different problems involving one dog, although the average is just over two different problems per dog.

Many problems are related to each other and with a great number of these problems a course of basic control training will automatically eliminate them.

My own experience indicates that the following undesirable situations cause the owners the greatest inconvenience:

1. Dogs pulling on the lead or generally being uncooperative while out walking with the owner.
2. Dogs not coming back to the owner when called after being given a period of freedom.
3. Dogs jumping up on the owner, family or visitors.
4. Dogs being destructive, particularly in the home or the car.
5. Dogs being aggressive to people or other dogs under varying circumstances.

Although most problems can be put into specific categories, each difficult situation is of major concern to the individual dog owner who is affected by it. He is not really interested in statistics or that his own problem is not unique, although there can be some consolation in knowing that other dog owners are having their lives disrupted by similar difficulties.

Some behaviour problems being discussed may well appear to be repetitive but a difference in location or circumstances can create a change in approach. The cause of these problems may be the same but the remedial action can often be quite different.

There are certain basic codes which are considered essential to obtain and maintain a balanced response from a dog. It is often said that an owner must start off in the manner in which he wishes to continue. This is perfectly true and it should always be in an owner's mind that consistency in approach with any dog and in any situation is very important.

However, consistency should never be so constrictive that it affects a dog's adaptability to the variation in circumstances he will experience throughout his life. We can now look at two simple applications of the basic code 'a dog owner must start as he means to go on', and very briefly consider the practicalities of the situations.

A puppy's place in a car is on or behind the back seat. From the day the puppy is picked up from the breeding kennel that is where he is put.

This dictum implies that cuddling or comfort for the puppy is ill-advised as the puppy will expect such treatment every time he is in the car and he must become accustomed to his proper place when travelling.

Although theoretically correct the behaviourists who advocate this practice have made no allowance for the stress factors in taking a puppy away from the protection afforded by the presence of his mother or the collective company of his litter mates.

A puppy has been run on by the breeder for a show career and has known no other sleeping quarters than his kennel. At the age of eighteen months it has become obvious that he will not make the top grade and is sold to a family.

Sleeping quarters, eating habits, environment and companions have all changed in the time it took to write and hand over a cheque.

The dog has obviously been out in a car to go to shows and travelling to his new home is not too much of an ordeal, but where is he going to sleep when he gets to his new home? The stress factor is likely to be great and if this is considered with the 'start as you mean to go on' policy it may prove to be too stressful for both the dog and the family.

However, these situations and others which are related will be fully discussed under the appropriate problem heading. It suffices at this stage to say that dogs, particularly young puppies, are susceptible to infection when they are under stress. It is more important during critical periods of change to minimise stress factors than to apply the 'start as you mean to go on' theory. The basic codes are there for guidance, to be used sensibly, not for blind obedience.

Life with a dog requires consideration and a certain amount of regimentation, but complete regimentation in the disciplined development of a dog's upbringing can create canine misery as well as taking the joy out of keeping a dog as a companion. In a young puppy stress due to a complete change of environment should not last more than a week. Although some puppies do not show any signs of stress and accept their new family straight away, it generally takes a few days for a puppy to adjust to and to adopt his new family. A loving, but sensible, approach during the period of adjustment will certainly create the start of a close mutual attachment.

There are certain important lessons a puppy will start to learn during that first week. He will learn who normally feeds him and will start to recognise the feeding routine. He will start to learn that toilet facilities are out in the garden. He will learn to recognise his bed, even if it is moved from one room to another from time to time. He will start to come back to his owner when called because of the pleasantness of the situation. These are all constructive learning habits which will affect the rest of his life.

During that first week there are other habits which can be avoided, habits which could eventually become problems. The puppy will not be encouraged to jump up for attention because members of the family will get down to his level to fondle him and visitors will be urged to do likewise. He will have no thoughts of getting on to a chair for love and affection (he is not yet big enough to try) because it will be given at floor level. The family will either kneel or sit on the floor beside the puppy to give him a few minutes of comfort. Being a lap dog at this early age, particularly with smaller breeds of dogs can become a habit which may well result in a number of aggression or possessive problems. With larger breeds the problems may differ slightly: a German Shepherd Dog or a Rottweiler cannot curl up on the owner's lap but he can take possession of the chair.

It should be recognised

- that once a canine action has taken place, be it good or bad, it is likely to be repeated under similar circumstances.
- if that action is repeated under similar circumstances it will most likely become a habit.
- the development of a habit under certain circumstances can easily develop further to cover a variety of circumstances.

Avoiding situations which cause problems may be termed as a defeatist approach to the question, but there are many occasions when it is more practical to avoid a problem until training or conditioning has created the required amount of control or a change in the behaviour pattern. There are other occasions when the best policy is to avoid certain situations completely.

If a dog chases a jogger, or children, even in fun, these situations should be avoided until proper control has been attained. If a dog chews the mail when it comes through the letter box, a cage can be fitted to catch the mail and keep it secure from the destructive attention of the dog.

It must be recognised that every time a dog has the opportunity to behave in a manner which is not in keeping with the requirements of the owner the progress of correction will generally take much longer. At other times such lapses can completely nullify the effects of corrective training.

Some problems become confirmed habits and it can take time to stop these undesirable recurrences completely. A remedy should become effective in the very first instance that it is used and on all the following occasions when it is applied. In many cases a failure on the part of the owner to maintain the corrective or preventive approach will encourage lapses into the old bad habits. It is, therefore, up to the owner to ensure that any lapses are not considered to be the failure of the remedy or irresponsibility on the dog's part, but a breakdown of his own ability to assess the degree of consolidation required to eliminate the problem completely.

Sympathy can help to turn an unpleasant experience into a confirmed problem for the future. Children who meet up with a very minor accident and turn to an adult for comfort and sympathy and get it will soon learn that it is right and proper to make a fuss over a minor situation. However, if the child's mind is pleasantly and excitedly diverted from the effects of the unpleasant situation he will soon forget that it happened. Dogs are no different. The dam of a litter will bark at an intruder and have the puppies scurrying back to the nest for protection – to their tiny minds that is the correct thing to do.

If an owner gives protection and sympathy to a puppy or adult dog every time something unpleasant happens the dog will think it is right and proper to seek this protection: sympathy is the strongest form of protection. However, if a dog's mind is diverted from the effect of this unpleasantness by fun and excitement the matter will soon be forgotten and the problem will fail to materialise.

In the following chapters many basic problems appear in a number of variations and from the owners of all types of dogs, from various breeds and mixtures of breeds. However, some of these problems are more prevalent in particular breeds and where this happens the particular breed or breeds are specifically mentioned. Other behaviour problems can be age-related and in these instances the age group also receives a specific mention.

Every effort has been made to help dog owners associate their problems with the situations being discussed and where possible references are made between problems to ensure that maximum benefit can be obtained.

CHAPTER FIVE

Problems in the Home

Most problems originate in the home. Some are contained within the four exterior walls and some spill out into the garden and may affect the immediate neighbourhood, while others spread out to cover the general environment which will then affect the community at large.

Dogs who jump up on the family are likely to jump up on acquaintances or friends they meet in the street. Dogs who are aggressive towards postmen or others when separated by the front door or a pane of glass may follow through with that aggressiveness on meeting a uniformed person while out for a walk. A dog who hides under the bed because he has been found carrying out some misdemeanour will learn quickly to ignore calls for his return when out enjoying the freedom of his exercise area.

A lack of control in the home, destructive or dirty habits may be considered by some dog owners to be their special secret; nobody needs to know the problems they have to contend with when they occur within the confines of the home, especially when they are prepared to forego the pleasure of receiving visitors. It can be their cross to bear. However, these problems will show themselves one way or another when the dog is taken out in the car, for a walk, to the vet, or to visit friends.

It is important, therefore, that every problem in the home is treated seriously, with action being taken to avoid problematic situations. When problems already exist measures must be put into operation to create a more harmonic existence between dog and owner.

Dogs and owners are most often together in the home, and problems in that area can only impair their companionship. Dogs are with their owners primarily and principally as companions, and the friendship between them can only be truly enjoyed if dogs respect their owners and owners act in a manner which will earn that respect.

Problem 5.1 – BRINGING HOME A NEW PUPPY

Many years ago we brought home an eight-week-old puppy from the breeder. This was his first journey in a car; he was very sick and made quite a mess of my clothes and the car. We are now thinking about getting a replacement puppy and would like to avoid this sickness in the car.

An Understanding and Probable Causes

There is probably a combination of causes but the fundamental cause could be stress. The puppy is leaving his mother and litter mates, also the only home and human faces (or scents) he has ever really known. He is under stress, he needs comforting and reassurance. He has to contend with the motion of the car and the effect this may have on his last meal, which will still be in his stomach.

These are the principal causes but to what degree does each factor contribute to the problem? There is no straight answer to that question, as the story of three German Shepherd puppies from the same litter illustrates. They were Duich, Drambuie and Duncan. Duich was picked up by his new owner and was driven some 300 miles to North Wales. He was sick once within the first couple of miles but was never sick again during that journey or any subsequent journey. Drambuie was to live in Essex and was delivered by the breeder to his new owner at Wetherby, about half-way. The puppy was on the back seat beside the breeder while a friend looked after the driving. This was a journey of more than 200 miles and the puppy was sick within the first mile and then repeatedly sick during the next 120 miles or so. Drambuie was transferred to his new owner, given a light meal and a drink, but was free of sickness during the other 200 mile journey to his new home; he has never been sick in the car since. The breeder kept Duncan and he was intermittently sick on local journeys until he was about eight months of age, but is now an excellent traveller. There can be no guarantee that puppy sickness can be avoided during the journey home.

REMEDIAL AND PREVENTIVE ACTION YOU CAN TAKE

There are details to be considered if the possibility of puppy sickness on that first journey home is to be reduced and there are also essential preparations to assist in coping with sickness if it does occur.

A considerate breeder will refrain from feeding a puppy before you go to collect him. It is preferable to collect the puppy just before his normal feeding time. He may be too miserable to appreciate that he is missing a meal and if he settles to the journey all right, little pieces of digestive biscuits may well take his interest. If he has been sick, with no indications of a repeat performance, you also may feel it worthwhile to give him pieces of biscuit.

Discuss the planned new arrival with your vet and accept his advice on whether a sedative should be considered before the journey and take any other advice he may be kind enough to offer.

Do not wear your best clothes when you go to collect your puppy. Take old towels and newspapers or a kitchen towel roll. Always be prepared for sickness. Take a box and a blanket for him to settle into, but you may well finish up with him on your lap.

The driver must give consideration to his new charge: fast cornering or speed on rough roads can make the difference between a contented puppy or a sick one. Car suspension which is too soft or too firm can make a difference but the effect of driving conditions can be minimised by suitable padding under the puppy, even if it is just the passenger's lap.

It is an important day for you and your puppy. Break as many rules as you wish so long as everything is done in the puppy's best interest to ease the transition.

Problem 5.2 – A PUPPY'S FIRST FEW NIGHTS IN THE NEW HOME

I am buying my first puppy and have heard from friends about the cries of distress from a new puppy settling in at night and I am getting completely conflicting advice on how to handle the situation.

An Understanding

There are many ways of settling a new puppy into a peaceful nightly routine and this can be combined with house training to help minimise the period of soiling in the house, particularly overnight.

As already mentioned, puppy stress due to the dramatic change of environment should be given prime consideration. Everything possible should be done during the first few days (and nights) to make the puppy feel at home and to completely counteract the temporary stressful mental condition.

How this situation is going to be tackled may depend on where the puppy is finally going to have his permanent sleeping quarters. That does not mean to say that you must make the choice on the first night and stick to it.

I recall speaking to a police dog handler about his new young charge. This handler and a colleague ('Bill' and 'John') both received replacement eight-week-old German Shepherd puppies who were litter brothers. The day following the puppies' first night in their new homes Bill asked John, 'Any problems with your puppy last night?'

John replied, 'None at all, we had a very quiet night. What about you?'

Bill responded, 'We had a very bad night with the puppy crying most of the time.'

John asked, 'Where did your puppy sleep?'

Bill answered, 'Out in the kennel, where did yours sleep?'

John replied, 'In bed between my wife and myself.'

This is a true story and it shows two extremes in thought and consideration. As adult police dogs both of these puppies finished by sleeping in their respective kennels by day or by night, depending on the handlers' various shifts.

I have known of puppies spending their first few weeks in their own bed in the bedroom at night and then being transferred to the kitchen or outdoor kennel without difficulty. With more than one new puppy, I have spent the first few nights sleeping on a camp bed in the vicinity of the kitchen with or close to the puppy and responding to his calls of nature to take him outside whenever necessary. I then transfer myself to the bedroom and leave a contented puppy to sleep in the kitchen on his own. Later he can be moved to an outdoor kennel without difficulty.

SETTLING-IN PROCEDURE

A suitable bed is most important. With an eight-week-old puppy a large cardboard box, big enough to allow for a few weeks' growth, suitably cut and with bedding is quite satisfactory. If it is intended to go to the expense of purchasing a bed at this stage, make sure that it is big enough for a full-grown dog. We inherited a polyurethene moulded bed which is suitable for a German Shepherd puppy and it is continually being lent out to friends when they get new puppies.

The bed must always be available for the puppy to go into when he is ready for a sleep and he should be encouraged to make good use of it. The box in itself is not of lasting importance but the bedding should always have at least one item with the puppy's scent on it.

Although young puppies seem to sleep most of the time, a period of activity before they go to bed overnight will certainly help them get into the habit of going to sleep without receiving physical contact from their owners. Constant physical contact should be avoided. John, the police dog handler, got away with it, but his expertise and judgement were probably accountable. Although a period of activity before going to bed is advisable, no puppy should be expected to settle down for the night while he is still 'high' from excitement.

A cleaned out marrow bone can keep a puppy occupied for a while before he drops off to sleep last thing at night. Put a good smear of meat paste, spreading cheese or some such appetising treat well inside the marrow bone and a puppy can spend some time trying to get into the last morsel of food. Each day the bone can be cleaned out by passing boiling water through the centre to make it ready for the next application. This same approach with the marrow bone can be used at any time as an initial comforter when the puppy is being left alone.

I have found that three nights can settle a puppy into sleeping on his own in the kitchen without my company:

First night – in the kitchen with him.
Second night – next door in the dining room beside the open door, but with a low barrier in the doorway.
Third night – in the dining room with the door closed.
Fourth night – back in my own bed upstairs.

An older dog in the house can help a youngster to settle in, but there can come a time when they must be separated and, although I normally have an older dog in the house, the puppy is initially expected to sleep at night without the company of the older dog. Although it is not essential to keep the puppy and the older dog separate at night during the initial period, it does help to create some independence from the start.

If a puppy is to spend his first week or two in his own bed in your bedroom, then his daytime sleeping should be mainly in the room which is going to be his principal sleeping quarters. If he does not get accustomed to daytime sleeping out of your company he will not accept overnight exclusion from your presence without complaint. Again the use of the filled marrow bone can be an excellent comforter.

To sleep in the kennel overnight requires the same approach. Get your puppy accustomed to sleeping in the kennel during the daytime before introducing the overnight routine.

Problem 5.3 – HOUSE TRAINING

I have a four-month-old puppy whom I brought home when he was eight weeks old. He is still wetting most nights and sometimes during the day.

An Understanding and Probable Causes

The understanding is based on the fact that a puppy, at some time and in some place, requires to relieve both his bladder and his bowels. Initially, these needs are often, but gradually as he gets older they become less frequent.

A puppy will relieve himself as needs demand and will make use of any area that takes his fancy. The one area which is not normally used for his toilet requirements is his bed. He may perform just outside it. However, if he has been penned in his sleeping quarters during part of his short life and could not get out of his bed to perform, he may not be too fussy if his bed is wet or not.

It might appear that I have just stated the obvious, but it is the failure to fully appreciate the obvious which causes most of the problems. This results in neglecting the opportunities to ensure that the puppy utilises the areas of your selection at the times which are more important to him. The more often a puppy is given the opportunity to relieve himself where he wants the more difficult it will be to control his toilet requirements to the areas which suit the owner. When control is achieved for the place of convenience, the dog will exert some control over the timing of these events.

A puppy generally wishes to relieve himself immediately after waking up and after he has had a meal. It is crucial that these periods be observed and utilised to ensure that the puppy is in the right place for his toilet requirements at these times. A puppy can often be seen wandering around at odd times and then squatting to gain relief. Vigilance is required to anticipate a puppy's requirements and prompt action by the owner will generally prevent an accident.

A puppy will be drawn to utilise the general or specific area he has used in the past. This may be the kitchen floor or a rug in the hall; it could be a purposely placed newspaper or an area in the garden. If scent from previous usage is there, be it by accident or by the owner's design, the attraction will draw him to the area when the need arises and the opportunity is available.

It should also be appreciated that a happy puppy is easier to train than an unhappy one. A puppy which is continually being punished or chastised for any reason, but particularly as a result of a toilet accident, is going to be an unhappy one and may well be very unsure of himself. This will cause stress and uncertainty in coping with situations he cannot understand.

REMEDIAL AND PREVENTIVE ACTION YOU CAN TAKE

The initial objective is to control the place where the puppy is given the opportunity to relieve himself. He may be a very young puppy or a puppy who has been allowed to get into the habit of relieving himself where he wishes.

The newspaper as a moveable toilet area in the house has been widely recommended in many books and it is certainly a method that gets results. The principle is to start by spreading newspaper around outside the puppy's bed area and to note where he actually performs. A small piece of soiled paper can be put between two pages of paper to be used as a replacement and placed in the spot as an inducement to perform in the same place. This permits a reduction in area covered by the paper. A sheet of plastic under the newspaper should prevent any soiling from getting on to the floor, especially if this is carpetted. The newspaper can be moved gradually towards the outside door. Once the puppy has been conditioned to go to the door, it is then easy to get him outside to perform.

However, if an owner becomes too dependent on newspapers and neglects vigilance or the natural timing of a puppy's toilet requirements the desirable results will take a long time to attain.

If newspaper is being used in the house or if an accident has to be cleaned up with a piece of kitchen roll, a soiled piece can be put into the garden in an area close to the back door. A little earth can be put on top of the paper to prevent it from being blown away. The smell of the puppy's urine or faeces in the area will help to induce the desirable performances when he is taken out.

A young puppy cannot be expected to go through the whole night without requiring to relieve himself. By sleeping beside him a light-sleeping owner can get the puppy outside to the place of convenience before an accident can happen. However, very few owners are prepared or able to operate such a routine.

Some owners use a play-pen or indoor kennel for a puppy to sleep in during his daytime naps or overnight. This area should be big enough to contain a sleeping area and an area covered by newspaper or the like for toilet requirements. During the day the puppy is likely to make his way back to his sleeping quarters to make use of the newspaper. Vigilance ensures that you catch him in time and get him outside quickly to perform in the area of your choice.

Getting a puppy outside as quickly as possible is essential. If necessary, and especially during the first week or two, he can be picked up and carried out, but it is much better if you can get his attention. Use any pleasurable means at your disposal. Your tone of voice and your actions, even the help of a handy play toy can divert his thoughts from his toilet requirements for sufficient time to allow you to get him to follow you outside.

When you get him outside and in the area containing the scents from previous performances you should blend into the background and scenery. If you have used a toy as an inducement to go outside let him play with it, but do not play with him. The toy was his reward for coming out but if you do nothing he will soon get bored with the situation and turn his attention to more pressing needs.

You should only speak when the puppy is actually performing to tell him quietly that he is a clever or a clean boy. Let him know you are pleased and then give him more attention if you wish.

You may have thoughts of leaving your puppy outside on his own to relieve himself. It could be raining or there could be a good programme on television; the temptation to leave the puppy to his own devices will be strong – but what effect will your departure have on the puppy? He will probably want to come inside and his mind will be occupied with these thoughts instead of the business at hand. You will not know if he has performed and will let him in to do his toilet on the kitchen floor. If he has performed while you are in the house you have missed an opportunity to praise him at the correct time and have therefore lost a training opportunity.

Overnight accidents are another matter. Here patience, under-standing and planning are the principal considerations. Babies cannot go through the night without a wet nappy: even when they become toddlers and have been potty-trained during the day, nappies are still required at night. This factor should be given consideration when puppies have overnight accidents.

Factors which will help or hinder overnight cleanliness include

contentment, tiredness, feeding, liquid intake and duration. Contentment comes with a relaxed puppy who is happy to go to bed for the
night. Tiredness can go with contentment, but a puppy who sleeps
all evening, is let out into the garden to perform, then put to bed
when fully awake and not in the least bit tired may not have a full
night's sleep. However, an over-excited puppy being put to bed is
likely to create other problems before settling down for the night.
The timing of the puppy's last meal and the amount of liquid intake
will also affect your pleasure or disappointment in the morning.
With this in mind, advice from your vet specifically suited to your
own dog can be safer than any general but well-meaning comments.
Duration is also very important, especially when some owners with
young puppies expect to be able to take a long lie-in at the week-ends.

First movements in the house in the morning can waken a puppy
and prompt him to relieve himself before you get to him after you
have washed and dressed. Getting out of bed and going straight to
the puppy's sleeping quarters to let him out can prevent disappointment. I have often wondered how often a single pool on the floor
was caused by the owner getting up at five o'clock in the morning
to attend to his own toilet requirements. The noise and vibration of
somebody walking across the hall to the toilet or the flush itself
may be sufficient to waken and activate a puppy.

Any accident, by day or by night, should be cleaned with a
strong disinfectant to minimise any residual scent and reduce the
possibility of that area attracting a repeat performance.

It is your own dedication which creates success and not the
puppy's fault when accidents do occur.

Problem 5.4 – DESTRUCTIVE DOGS

*My young dog is now about a year old and he is very destructive when
left on his own. He will chew any slippers, shoes, or even books, if they
are within his reach. As a young puppy his chewing concerned me but I
was told it was only teething and he would grow out of it. I am afraid I
took that advice and it has caused me a lot of trouble and expense.*

AN UNDERSTANDING AND PROBABLE CAUSES

Dogs who destroy household or personal effects by chewing probably create the most expensive problem in the field of domestic ownership. One expensive shoe with teeth marks will ruin a pair. A small section of floor covering being given the incisor treatment will require a full replacement at considerable cost – and the likelihood of a recurrence cannot be discounted. Wallpaper can be torn from the walls, and skirting boards full of teeth marks with unseemly splinters on the floor create the need for redecorating. The variations are endless – with some dogs nothing seems to be safe.

The causes of this type of problem are also numerous. A continuation of the natural desire to chew during the teething period is probably the most significant factor, but stress, boredom, diet and hyperactivity are other factors which require consideration. Whatever the contributing factor, the opportunity to chew must also be a conditional feature.

It is certainly correct to expect chewing during a puppy's period of teething. Chewing cannot and should not be stopped during that period but it should be controlled to ensure that only certain permitted items are available for chewing.

Puppies or dogs who object to being left on their own are going to be in a stressful situation and chewing may become a canine reaction which is countering the effect of stress; this again can become a habit. At times the stress is caused by punishment received for previous 'offences'.

Boredom creates its own problems. A puppy or dog with little or nothing to do is like a child. The brain is developing and seeks its own form of activity if it is not put to constructive use.

Some diets can be deficient in nutrients which are necessary for a balanced and healthy dog. Chewing of certain items may be caused by the dog's need to supplement his dietary intake. It is often felt that stripping and eating wallpaper is caused by the desire for the wallpaper adhesive. I am more inclined to think that at times a loose piece of wallpaper has taken a bored dog's attention and it has ripped off easily. This can be the start of an occupational time filler.

Hyperactivity can be caused by an unbalanced diet or the

inclusion of certain additives in the diet. There is little known about the dietary causes of hyperactivity, although a very high protein diet can be a principal factor. I recall one case where a Labrador cross had destroyed the kitchen floor covering and then demolished the replacement. This young dog was hyperactive and on investigation into its diet, it was revealed that he was fed scrambled eggs at least four days a week, and five at one time: at least twenty eggs a week into *one* dog! The eggs were stopped and in a short time hyperactivity dropped and destructive chewing ceased. We normally give our German Shepherd Dogs two eggs per week and have no problems. It has also been thought that milk in a dog's diet can cause hyperactivity. It would seem that no two dogs are the same and a particular type of feeding can suit one dog but not another.

Children can produce hyperactivity in a young dog and that again may cause chewing tendencies, but more about dogs and children appears in Chapter Nine.

To try to take corrective action after the event is of no value and sound preventive measures before a possible event can save a lot of heartache and expense.

REMEDIAL AND PREVENTIVE ACTION YOU CAN TAKE

As with so many problems the remedies and preventive actions are identical: they both require vigilance and attention to detail until a puppy or young dog has become accustomed to the rules of the house. In thirty years or more of having dogs in the house and each one as a young puppy, we have had three items chewed by various youngsters. One youngster chewed our daughter's library book and a wooden training dumbbell (belonging to the older dog) and another youngster decided to chew my original copy of *Training the German Shepherd Dog*. In each instance it was our own fault for leaving these items lying around during the teething period.

During a chewing period it is important that vigilance and tidiness are of prime consideration. A quiet puppy is either sleeping or up to some mischief on his own and if he is in a position to chew indiscriminately he will do so. Observation is the name of the game. He does not require watching every minute of this active period but you should always be aware of what is going on.

Tidiness means more than having everything in its place. Knitting on the bottom shelf of an occasional table is a strong temptation and any small ornaments at the fireplace are fair game for an inquisitive puppy. It is like having a little toddler visit the house: many a grandmother will clear the decks in readiness for a visit from a bright-eyed little grandchild. Doors should also be kept closed. Little puppies like to investigate underwear, slippers and the like, finding their way into a quiet corner for a chew.

Many experts say that old slippers or socks should not be given to a puppy as toys to chew and play with. Because of the owner's scent on these items it is said that a puppy does not know the difference between a play slipper and the slippers in daily use. I have never found this to be a problem because during the chewing period the slippers in use are never left for the puppy to find. If a new toy is given to a puppy and played with, his own scent is on it and he will quickly recognise that the items bearing his scent belong to him and eventually that similar items without his scent are not his to play with.

A multitude of toys is part of the answer and, like children, a puppy will always welcome a new toy. Toys can be bought but some of the most prized possessions are thrown out containers such as well-washed plastic squeezy bottles. An old sock or two and an old cardigan (without buttons or zip) can give much pleasure and when these items have served a short but useful life they can be thrown out and replaced by others.

A large box is a necessity and should be placed where the puppy can rummage for his favourite toy of the day. A cardboard box from the supermarket is good enough and if that gets chewed it can be replaced. We have counted over twenty toys in a box at one time. At the moment we have two dogs at home – and the youngster is under two years of age – and there are twelve toys in their toy box: three balls, a squeaky toy, a piece of blanket, two rubber kongs, a squeezy bottle, a metal Dinky Toy, an old check chain, a bunch of keys and a rubber ring. Some toys were bought and others picked up in the course of time. As the youngster is well past the destructive chewing stage there is no longer the variety of toys to demolish but some or all get dragged out most evenings.

In the environment just discussed correction should now be

considered when a youngster is caught in the act of chewing a forbidden item. To scold or take any punitive action after the event is worse than useless. It may get the feeling of anger out of your system but it will not prevent a recurrence.

Constructive training, even with a young puppy, should be applied to cover the first and second targets of the attention-getting routine in Chapter Two. Two or three sessions daily and each covering up to half a minute will show remarkable effect after a few days and with some puppies a single day will be sufficient. With this very elementary stage of training the foundation is set for gaining your puppy's attention at any time while in the house.

Whenever you observe your puppy looking at a forbidden item or actually chewing it use his name and immediately follow through with 'NO' or 'BAA'. Although volume is not necessary the voice should be very penetrating. The instant you receive the youngster's full attention give him praise and stay where you are. This praise may lead him to believe that he can return to the object of his destructive interest and it will require a repeat of your verbal *stopper*. If you move towards the youngster you may start to lay the foundation of fear and it is important that fear be avoided. Whenever you gain his full attention call him to you, get down on to the floor – you can sit, kneel, or lie on your stomach – and give him every encouragement to come to you for praise or reward if you have had the opportunity to get some form of reward to hand. The reward can be a titbit or one of his toys to play with or chew. The reason for getting down on to the floor is to reduce your apparent size and to look much less domineering.

If you have a young dog who already runs away, with or without the forbidden item, try getting down to floor level and if that is not effective make use of the short line. The six foot short line has already been mentioned in Chapter One. The line has a clip on one end, and is free of knots or has a loop on the other end. If the line is attached while the youngster is in the house it cannot get caught under a door or elsewhere. However, a trailing line should never be attached to an unattended dog. To leave a dog at home unattended with an attached line could finish with some unexpected disaster.

If the puppy is stubborn or runs away, the end of the short line can be picked up and the attention-getting routine at the second target can be applied.

An unattended dog can have many opportunities to chew and destroy. If the items being destroyed are furniture or fixtures the answer must be to change the conditions. An indoor or outdoor kennel could be the answer and the use of this facility is described in detail under Problems 5.10 and 9.4.

Problem 5.5 – DOGS WHO DO NOT WISH TO BE LEFT ALONE

My dog will not let me go out of his sight without whining or barking. Although I do not go out to work and give him my company most of the time, going shopping or visiting creates problems. He will bark continually, scratch the door and if he can find any item of my clothing he will chew and destroy it. The neighbours are now objecting to the disturbance he creates.

An Understanding and Probable Causes

Pet dogs who spend the greater part of their lives in the house with their owners do not like being left behind, but there is no reason why they should not accept the situation as a way of life. The majority of dogs will accept being left at home, even if they would prefer to be with their owners. These dogs will settle to their periods of isolation and cause no trouble, although they may give a protective bark if somebody comes into the garden or to the door of the house. They then settle back to their period of isolated contentment. The question now is – why do so many dogs act differently?

Stress is the principal cause of this type of problem, although dominance and the failure to get their own way may be at the root of the stress factor with some dogs.

Many puppies are brought up to expect a great deal of personal attention. From the earliest days they are allowed to follow the owner round the house and into the garden, and every waking moment of these youngsters is spent beside the owner. I have heard many a person say that they cannot even go to the bathroom without the dog demanding to be with them. During the owners' periods of relaxation the dog is either on the chair or settee with them or lying at their feet and probably maintaining body contact.

Little dogs who are carried round by their owners are particularly prone to this problem. They continually desire to follow this owners or to be carried. Combined with the excessive body contact this will certainly create stress problems when the owners go out of sight or leave their dogs at home on their own.

Quite a number of owners who work all day feel that they must salve their consciences and make up for canine loneliness by encouraging the puppies or more mature dogs to follow them round or to maintain body contact. This is also true of some people who have taken on rescue dogs. Because of bad treatment (real or imaginary) from previous owners the new owners feel that they must make up for the misdeeds of others. There is no moderation, the dog is treated like a spoilt child and can do no wrong. He is actually encouraged to become completely dependent on the new owner and within a short time this dependency becomes a very troublesome burden.

Another principal cause of problems relating to leaving a dog on his own is the tremendous excitement many owners create when they return home. The dog is excited and the owner makes him even more excited trying to make up for the fact that he had to leave the dog at home. To a well-balanced dog with no stress or dominance problems this situation is of no real consequence, but to the dog with the problems being discussed this situation can only generate greater canine desire for continuous company.

Situations involving constant attachment create two extremes which most dogs cannot handle. They are not mentally equipped for total uninhibited companionship when periods of isolation must come into their lives at some time. The owner becomes a slave to his dog by creating a form of canine dominance which will dictate the terms of the companionship.

REMEDIAL ACTION YOU CAN TAKE

It is essential that body or close contact be minimised, that your dog is not allowed to follow you wherever you go and that he is taught to become more independent. This may not be easy and it can take quite some time to achieve success. There are various cures to this problem which are recommended and some are successful with a few dogs, but these so-called cures do not take the stress factor into consideration and they can even cause greater stress problems. The process of rehabilitation must be carried out gradually and any situation which closely resembles the pattern of events which causes the problem should be avoided when possible. Each recurrence of a problem will lengthen the period of correction.

Many dogs get excited when their owners start preparing to go out – putting on a pair of shoes is sufficient to trigger off canine excitement. They expect to go out, so when they are then left behind they whine or bark to show their objection. Any attempt to go back to make them stop being noisy, no matter how unpleasant you make it, is giving the dog the attention he wants. This is generally of little value. However, a well-balanced dog who starts to act in this manner, possibly because of unusual circumstances, may well react favourably to a few choice words telling him to be quiet. It is worth trying but it is not worth wasting a lot of time on this suggestion.

The process of rehabilitation is based on the combination and progression of objectives which can be developed quite separately. The overall objective is to eliminate the stress factor and create general canine contentment while you and your dog are apart so that the distance and period of separation can be increased without undue concern on the part of the dog.

The principal objectives are:

1. Developing a *contented* sit and stay while you leave your dog for a short period and distance.
2. Eliminating lengthy periods of body contact. Contact for a few seconds at a time and as a reward for some controlled response is recommended.
3. Creating out-of-bounds areas within the home so that you may carry out your daily functions without being followed everywhere.
4. Creating limited access to the garden when you go out of the house for very short periods. This must not affect the dog's natural toilet requirements.
5. Ignoring your dog when you rejoin him after (3) or (4) until your presence no longer evokes his excited attention.

Objective 1
Developing a contented sit and stay while you leave your dog for a short period.
The fourth and fifth targets of the training routine of Chapter Two provide the focus of your objective and the fifth target is particularly relevant where enthusiastic praise can be given without your dog moving from the sit position.

Without a calm and composed stay while you are within a lead's length of your dog the stress factor is unlikely to be eliminated and it is important that time and effort be spent on these targets to achieve a satisfactory response from your dog.

Each time your dog is left for this very short period and distance you should go back and stand beside him for about five seconds before letting him know he can move. He should not be allowed to move until he is given permission. The best way of releasing your dog from this stay position is to take a quick side step from him with the pleasant expression 'O.K. son'.

As soon as you have given your dog permission to move, walk away from him and ignore him completely. Sit on a chair if this is available and maintain an indifferent attitude. Your dog is likely to be excited and want attention but do not show any response, do not touch him or even create eye-to-eye contact until he settles. When he has settled recognition of your pleasure can be given. A quick sit, a little pat or a stroke with 'That's a good boy' is sufficient, then break the sit as before.

During the training period it should be possible to create more than a lead's distance between your dog and yourself, but if this method is carried out it must be based on 100 per cent success. *Your dog must not move from the designated spot.* It may be possible to leave your dog in one room while you can go into another with the door left open so that you can watch and chat to him. Do not call your dog to you, always go back to him and finish as before. Although it is not essential to move more than a lead's distance from your dog for this objective, this can form a useful development which will help with overall control and stability.

The training to the standard you require should be carried on and consolidated until all five objectives have created the end result you are looking for. If you have difficulty in achieving this objective it may be advisable to attend a dog training class which is controlled by a knowledgeable and considerate instructor.

Objective 2
Eliminate lengthy periods of body contact.
This is not a purposeful training routine but is principally a case of reducing the amount and length of time in contact with your dog. The process to be applied depends on the present amount and type of contact there is with your dog. If your dog is normally allowed to be on your lap, this must be stopped; the same if he lies on the settee beside you, or if he lies at your feet but insists on maintaining body contact.

The process of change can be gradual, contentment with the distance between you and your dog being your objective. This distance need not be great: some three to four feet from you creates a major breakthrough.

A blanket, cardigan, old jacket or some other suitable piece of material from his bed is the starting point; we shall, hereafter, call it the blanket. If he does not have such a blanket because he sleeps on your bed at night, then pieces of blanket should be obtained. As a blanket requires washing from time to time, at least two pieces are required with both in the bed at the same time so that one can be taken away for washing. As your body scent as well as his own is going to be a comforter during this period, it can be helpful to sit on a washed blanket for a short spell before returning it to his bed.

Initially the blanket can be put where he normally lies. If it is on your lap or on the settee – so be it. After a couple of days of using the blanket on your lap or on the settee beside you with contact, put the blanket on the floor beside you. If you have a proper bed or basket for him, have this with the blanket right beside you. He must go on to the blanket and stay, instead of being on your lap or the settee. At first body contact can be maintained by touching or fondling him from time to time. You may wish to sit on the floor beside him until he settles to this routine. The use of a marrow bone as described in Problem 5.2 can be used initially, but only allow him to lick out the contents while on his blanket.

The development of Objective 1 can help to make your dog stay while you break physical contact and move three to four feet from him. Praise him while he is on the blanket and then when you release him ignore him completely.

In time you can tell your dog to go to his blanket instead of demanding body or close contact. If he normally sleeps on your bed at night, this should be allowed to continue until you have achieved success with daytime conditioning. However, bedtime separation may be rather difficult unless he is banned from the bedroom completely.

If he is banned from the bedroom at night – and this may be necessary to achieve your full objective – Problem 5.2 for settling a puppy into a new home should be studied and applied. However, the period of conditioning is likely to take much longer than with a new puppy. It must be remembered that this is only part of the five objective plan.

Objective 3
Creating out-of-bound areas within the home.
You can ban your dog from coming upstairs with you or coming through to the bathroom or bedroom, but the areas chosen should be those which are used at intervals and for relatively short spells. A barrier may be helpful at first: it can be a piece of plywood, a baby gate, or a chair placed on its side across the entrance to the door.

When you go to the other side of the doorway with the barrier in place your dog is likely to try and jump over or go through it, depending on the type used and the size of dog. If your dog is over-excited and cannot be contained, withhold this procedure until Objective 1 has been accomplished. With a barrier in place the intention is not for your dog to sit and stay, but for him to be sufficiently controlled to remain calm.

It may be necessary to apply a little more training before you can leave your dog behind the barrier so that you can get on with the chores at hand. Allow your dog to maintain any position he wishes – standing, sitting or lying down – when you go to the other side of the barrier (or put it up behind you). Chat quietly to him but use an unpleasant 'NO' or 'BAA' if he tries to reach you.

Praise an agreeable response and only go back to him when he is accepting your conditions. When you go back ignore your dog for at least five seconds after he has calmly accepted your return.

Gaining the dog's attention, then changing from backward to forward movement.

Putting the dog into the sit position.

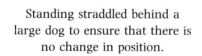

Standing straddled behind a large dog to ensure that there is no change in position.

Kneeling behind a small dog to ensure that there is no change in position.

Maintaining a small dog's attention when he sits in front.

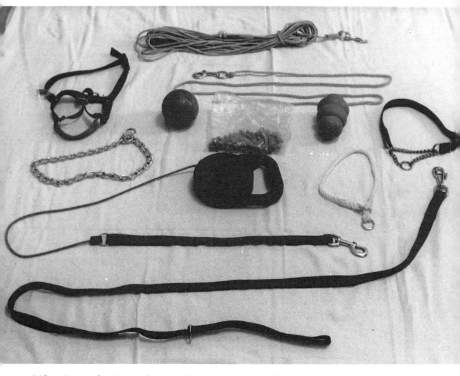

(*Above*) A selection of control equipment and training aids.

(*Below*) Use of the stop button on the flexi-lead to apply control.

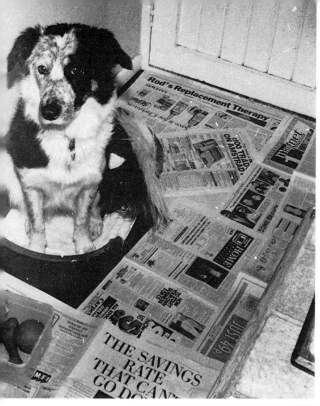

Spreading
newspapers
around the
puppy's bed is
one approach to
house training.

A toy box for a
puppy or an
active older dog.

(*Above*) Lead handling for training a dog to walk on a loose lead. (*Right*) The conventional method of holding the lead for normal walking with a control-trained dog.

Waving a walking stick in front of a dog's face to keep him in line.

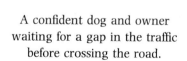

A confident dog and owner waiting for a gap in the traffic before crossing the road.

(*Left*) An indoor kennel that can also be used to advantage when travelling. (*Right*) An inner tailgate can be of great use too.

Well-constructed kennels and runs for two male dogs.

Make your dog sit and then praise him for sitting before you release him. Repeat this process until you feel that the barrier has become effective.

In due course, the barrier can be removed and the process repeated until this imaginary barrier has become effective. Doors can then be closed behind you with the same return procedure being applied – ignore your dog until he is calm, make him sit, then gentle praise.

Objective 4
Creating limited access to the garden.
Again this is just part of the process of letting your dog know that he cannot follow you as he pleases. This objective should be withheld until Objective 3 has been fully accomplished and the procedure in this instance is just the same: a barrier at the back door and conditioning to stay at the other side, with the build-up as utilised for indoor conditioning, and finally closing the back door to do a quick chore without encountering a stressful canine reaction. With effective indoor training this period of conditioning should take no more than a week or so.

As out of doors is not a banned area completely, your dog should also be taught to wait when the door is opened until you let him out. An excited dog should always be taught to give way to the owner and it may be advisable to put the lead on the dog to take him into the garden before releasing him until full conditioning has achieved the desired results. The attention-getting routine in Chapter Two creates the lead control which can be applied to ensure that you can influence your dog's actions or reactions.

Objective 5
Ignoring your dog when you rejoin him.
A significant factor in this problem is the encouraged excitement created by an owner when he comes home. This has already been discussed under Probable Causes.

The answer is to ignore your dog when he wants this initial burst of excited attention during the training and conditioning period for the four objectives already discussed. Whether you have gone into the next room or left your dog with a relative or friend while you go out shopping or for the evening, be blind and oblivious to his desire for attention. When he has calmed down, and if he is not beside you, call him in and make him sit for praise and a little affection before releasing him from the controlled situation.

Every time you leave your dog on his own before he has developed a less stressful or less dominant attitude he will continue to have this problem, which will at best delay the cure and at worst make your efforts ineffective.

If you do have to go out try to have a friend take your dog out for a walk before you prepare to leave and try to have him brought home before you. This will create an avoidance situation until you have attained a more balanced attitude between yourself and your dog. Remember to ignore your dog when you get home until he settles, then make him sit for a little praise and attention.

PREVENTIVE MEASURES YOU CAN TAKE

Prevention is based on an avoidance of canine stress or dominance. This does not mean that you cannot create unpleasant situations when they are required or that you should completely dominate your puppy or dog. Living with a dog is all about achieving a balanced approach and it may be advisable to revise the section in Chapter One relating to canine v human appreciation.

Creating a measure of independence also is of importance and the approach adopted with settling in a young puppy as discussed in Problem 5.2 is most appropriate. The very first indications of this problem with your dog should be countered by the remedial recommendations already described. Do not wait until the problem has got a great hold.

It will be recognised that many owners who have this problem have inherited canine stress or dominance. The dog may have been purchased beyond the small puppy stage from a breeding kennel when the change can be rather traumatic. The dog may have been sold because of the problems created by a previous owner, or it may be a rescue dog with very bad experiences from the past. In these cases the dog must be allowed to settle with as balanced an approach as is possible before remedial work can begin.

Note: An understanding of the remedies in this section will help you to achieve greater all-round control which will help prevent other problems from disrupting an otherwise pleasant canine companionship.

Problem 5.6 – JUMPING UP ON PEOPLE

I have a small dog, well past the puppy stage – in fact he is over two years of age – and he still keeps jumping up on me, various visitors at home or friends we meet in the street. This does not cause a real problem during dry and clean conditions but it does make clothes dirty when paws get wet or muddy.

An Understanding and Probable Causes

Dogs jump up on people for attention; it may be from excitement, stress or habit. Jumping up through dominance does not normally take place unless it is aggressively based. However, aggressively-based activities are dealt with under Chapter Eight, Aggression Problems, and are not considered to be part of the problem under discussion.

Although the problem is more prevalent with smaller dogs, medium to large dogs cannot be excluded. Some dogs are rather forceful as they jump up, but some of the larger dogs can be very gentle in the way they seem to stretch on their hind legs to gently place their front paws on a person's chest. There is a Rottweiler bitch I know who seems to glide up in an effortless and graceful movement without an ounce of pressure to give an appreciative lick, then expects to be given a titbit as a reward – she makes it very difficult to refuse.

Dogs who jump up for attention can knock children over and frighten them for life. They can also knock over the old and infirm, particularly when they are taken by surprise. With such falls injuries are easily sustained and broken bones can be difficult to mend – this is the more serious side.

However, on the subject of clothing, many a temper is lost because a clean dress or suit has been dirtied by muddy paws in an

overfriendly canine reception. Jumping up seems to be quite acceptable when the dogs are clean and casual clothing is the order of the
day, but unfortunately dogs do not know the difference and it is
this inconsistency which causes the problem. On one occasion the
dog is permitted, even encouraged, to jump up and the next he is in
trouble because the owner has changed into a good clean outfit.

The problem generally starts with puppies wanting attention or a
dog in distress receiving comfort. The owner's hands, eyes and
voice are the focal points for canine attention and affection. If these
focal points do not come down to the dog's level, the dog tries to get
up to these areas of attraction.

An owner's inconsistency and a failure to appreciate the results
of his own actions are the principal causes of dogs jumping up and
this then becoming a problem.

REMEDIAL ACTION YOU CAN TAKE

The remedies must start with consistency in not allowing your dog
to jump up on yourself or any other members of the family and in
preventing the dog from doing likewise with other people. This is
purposely put in two parts because the family at home must change
their ways, but you cannot expect the majority of visitors or people
you meet in the street to make similar changes.

As already mentioned the focal points of canine attention are
your hands, eyes and voice. Initially all three focal points should be
brought down and nearer to the dog's level. By kneeling there is no
need for him to jump up unless he is a very small dog. Your hands
should then become the principal focal point and you should use a
fondling approach. With this problem face-licking, carrying round
(small dogs) or any form of head-to-head affection should be
avoided. All affection should be shown through your hands and
backed up with a quiet but rewarding verbal contribution. At the
same time try to avoid eye-to-eye contact.

To achieve a permanent solution without having to kneel for
every welcome the fourth and fifth targets for the sit element of the
training routine in Chapter Two become essential. The initial training to achieve these targets may take a little time but the progression
of this training will enable you or the family to make your dog sit

before giving the fondling affection with the hands that will satisfy both you and your dog. If you also have problems when leaving your dog as discussed in Problem 5.5, then the routine of ignoring your dog until he settles after a parting should be applied. It may be advisable to study both problems to obtain the greatest advantage.

By making your dog sit for affection you are teaching a form of control which he requires. Although you are expected to stand in a reasonably upright position, it is more important that your hands can reach your dog's head and neck for fondling. With smaller dogs, this means bending down and closer to their level. Rather than bending right over the dog it is preferable to bend your knees until your hands are at the appropriate level.

There are more unpleasant methods which can be used and may achieve the desired end result, such as shouting at the dog, gripping his front feet when he jumps up, standing on his hind feet or even hitting his chest with your knee. All these methods when carried out correctly can be quickly effective, but if incorrectly applied and without the pleasant follow-up, they can create canine apprehension and this will then lead to other problems. The longer route to the goal helps to create a much better controlled situation.

If your dog jumps up on visitors to the home or acquaintances in the street, you must anticipate the situation. Initially it might be necessary to apply the training from the attention-getting routine in Chapter Two to the sixth target.

When approaching or being approached by an acquaintance with your dog on the lead, move backwards suddenly to take your dog's attention from the other person. Then move forward with your dog under your attentive control and with the training to the sixth target in mind he can be made to sit while you chat with the other person. If this person wishes to welcome and show affection to your dog he must be instructed to carry this out in the manner you have had to apply. Avoid eye contact, use hands at the appropriate level and speak in a quiet voice.

As training develops and greater control is attained the attention getting with backward movement will not be required. Simply make your dog sit when you meet up with an acquaintance. When control is fully established it may not be necessary to apply the lead or to make the dog sit but people must not apply a form of welcome which creates uncontrolled excitement from the dog, otherwise jumping up will be reintroduced.

When people visit your home put your dog on the lead and apply the same control as out in the street until training and conditioning have created a controlled response.

PREVENTIVE MEASURES YOU CAN TAKE

Preventive measures start with the new young puppy or an older one that has not yet been encouraged to jump up for attention and affection.

Keeping in mind the recommendations under Remedial Action, your hands and a soft, pleasant but unexciting voice are the focal points of your dog's attention. Your hands should be at a level which prevents the need for the puppy to jump up and a kneeling position is probably most appropriate. Eye-to-eye contact should not create a problem if your hands are used to fondle and control the puppy. Apply control to prevent jumping up by holding the puppy. A firm voice may be necessary if you have accidentally induced the situation through your own excitement.

Puppies who are brought up in this environment and are not encouraged from an early age never seem to think about jumping up for attention. Consistency and habit create the development of canine reactions – good or bad.

Problem 5.7 – DOGS AND FOOD

Food stealing is a real problem with my dog. He is a relatively large dog and can steal from the table or kitchen work top with ease. He is also quite a nuisance at meal times and whines if he is shut out of the dining area when we are eating.

AN UNDERSTANDING AND PROBABLE CAUSES

We start by assuming that the dog is receiving sufficient nourishment from his own food and it is not something lacking in his diet which is causing the problem. A visit to your vet may be advisable.

Some dogs are very greedy and others have no interest in food between their normal meal times. However, titbits of human food have been the ruination of many a dog.

This problem is normally created at an early age and two principal factors cause this complication to an owner's life. The first is the giving of titbits from the owner's plate, often compounded by teaching puppies to beg for those little tasty pieces which are intended for human consumption. The other is carelessly leaving food where the puppy or older dog can get at it. The problem may be caused by the type of titbits given previously; it can also be caused by giving the dog left-overs from a meal, particularly if the food is left on the owner's plate when it is given to the dog. The same can be said for giving dogs pots and pans to lick before washing up the dishes after a meal.

With many dogs giving them titbits or left-overs creates no such problem: this may well be due to the general approach to canine control and also where or when the titbits are given. Titbits from an owner or a member of the family while seated at the dining table will certainly create a problem at meal times. It only requires one member of the family to slip a tasty morsel to the dog to create canine attentiveness at every meal and the dog will not waste time sitting beside the members of the family who will not feed him if the guilty party is at the table.

Small children in the house can also cause the problem, especially a youngster learning to eat without parental help. A fair proportion of food will finish up on the floor to be cleaned up by the family pet.

The problem is based on taste discrimination: commercial dog food can seem to be lacking in appreciative taste when compared with food seasoned and prepared for human consumption. A taste for human food can make some dogs appear to be very fussy and indulgent owners can easily create a rod for their own backs by introducing their dogs to tasty morsels of this type.

Once the taste has been acquired, food left on the coffee table at a suitable height for the dog, or even on the kitchen work top, will be fair game and the dog will not consider himself to be a thief. He has been introduced to food he likes very much and will take every opportunity to help himself.

Kitchen rubbish bins can become a target for his desires – he may even learn how to open a cupboard or refrigerator door to get at the food he likes so much. The kitchen rubbish bin may contain the wrappings from butcher meat, egg shells or some other food-smelling items which take his interest: they are all items which may entice canine investigation.

REMEDIAL ACTION YOU CAN TAKE

Habits must change, titbits of your own food must stop and consideration should be given to limiting or even eliminating titbits of dog food, particularly during your own eating times. Withdrawal symptoms will become evident and your dog may become a bigger nuisance than the problem itself until a more balanced situation has been achieved.

A refusal to give a titbit, such as a biscuit at coffee time or a piece of meat from your dinner plate, when a dog asks for and expects to get it will cause bitter disappointment and continual pestering with the expectation that you will finally give in. It will be a case of his persistence against yours until one of you gives in.

From now on *all* food must be kept out of the dog's reach when he is not supervised. If it is necessary, control training must also take place and it is assumed that the recommended training in Chapter Two to create general control has been applied. Training the dog to go to his bed and stay there when told can be a great advantage and Objective 2 of Problem 5.5 can be applied effectively. The use of the marrow bone as described in Objective 2 and in Problem 5.2 can help to create a more settled situation. Remember that it is your dog's bone and the filling is human food (spreading cheese, etc.) and that it is a compromise until he can be told to go to bed and stay there for the period necessary without the inducement of a filled bone.

Whether you are preparing a meal or having a meal or a snack, put your dog into his bed for that period. Initially his filled marrow bone will help to satisfy him until this can be dispensed with. Your dog's bed does not necessarily have to be in some other part of the house and it will be easier to make the change if his bed is in the room with you during your feeding activities.

If you are careless and leave food accessible to your dog and then catch him thinking of helping himself or actually doing it, there is no sense in allowing him to continue. His attention must be diverted by calling his name with an instant follow-through of 'NO' or 'BAA'. The instant you gain his attention give him praise. The problem should be treated in the same way as for destructive dogs and as described in Problem 5.4. However, do not depend on this approach as your sole method of correcting the overall problem: it is of marginal long-term value.

A dog who has learnt to get into the kitchen rubbish bin is best countered by picking the bin off the floor and putting it out of reach when he has unsupervised freedom of the kitchen. If a dog knows how to open the refrigerator door to make his choice, then a chair or kitchen stool in front of the cabinet is likely to create an insurmountable problem for him.

Some dogs require a strong deterrent and a blown-up balloon can achieve such an objective. A balloon which bursts at a distance from your dog, but sufficiently close to instill dislike, will ensure that the dog will not go near balloons. A balloon tied to the refrigerator door or food cupboard will ensure that the dog will keep away from it. However, remedies of this nature always have side effects. During the festive season there are children's parties when there are balloons around and your dog will not have the opportunity of enjoying these festivities or the balloons will have to be barred and children will not be pleased with this idea.

Remedies of this nature cause a certain amount of stress or fear while your dog is in close proximity to the offending objects, but this is not a problem if he is given the opportunity to create distance between himself and the balloon.

Dogs who have become a nuisance with food as described in this section take time to cure. As already stated, there is a withdrawal period which will be stressful to the dog: he will not understand the changes in attitude and you, the owner, will find it difficult, but once the remedy has become effective meals can be taken in peace.

PREVENTIVE MEASURES YOU CAN TAKE

By studying the remedies just discussed the preventive measures should be quite evident. However, the most important factors are those of taste distinction and balanced control.

If your dog never tastes food which is prepared for humans he is unlikely to show interest in it. Any indication of canine interest is generally countered by ignoring the dog when he is attracted by the aroma of food. A dog who is given basic training and appreciates that he is not the pack leader will be much less likely to think about stealing your food.

Food should always be kept out of reach when the dog is not being supervised. Temptation should not be put in front of the dog, as even the best behaved dogs can be tempted if the conditions are right.

Problem 5.8 – DOGS ON FURNITURE

My fireside chair and my bed seem to have a special attraction for my dog. He is not allowed on either while I am at home but he is quite often caught curled up on my chair when there has been no one at home to supervise him and if the bedroom door has been left open it is evident that he has slept on the bed.

AN UNDERSTANDING AND PROBABLE CAUSES

This type of problem is not restricted to the simplicity of the case above. Many dogs can become very possessive over the chair, settee or bed of their choice and it can cause apprehension on the part of many owners to try to remove their dogs from the furniture. Some dogs can become rather aggressive through their possessiveness over a chair or some other piece of furniture and this factor requires the special attention which is described in Problem 8.2.

Quite often this problem starts with the puppy being allowed on the owner's lap, on the settee or on the bed at night. Some owners who enjoy a long lie-in at the week-end will let a puppy out to relieve himself and then will allow the puppy into the bedroom and on to the bed to salve their consciences. This can be the start of a habit which will give the puppy the feeling of a right to such comfort at times which suit him.

With some dogs it is the physical comfort of a chair or a bed which attracts them, with others it is the scent of their owners on the furniture which creates canine contentment.

Some owners have a special chair for the dog to occupy and they are not allowed on any other furniture. Often that chair is by a window so that the dog can watch the world go by. If this is what the owner wants and the dog sticks to the use of that one chair there is no problem. Nobody is complaining.

REMEDIAL ACTION YOU CAN TAKE

It will be apparent that consistency in your approach is very important. To be allowed on the chair or bed when he is clean and dry but to be in trouble for the same thing after coming in from the garden is not going to make sense to the dog. Clean or dirty, it makes no difference to him.

A dog who has received basic control training can easily be stopped in the act of getting on to the furniture and, generally, he will get off when told. Your remedial action may be principally that of control training but I would not expect this to be the full solution to the problem.

Scolding the dog when he is on the furniture is seldom of any value. It may get him off when he sees or hears you coming but it is unlikely to prevent him from jumping on to his chosen place of comfort altogether.

Avoidance of the situation is probably the best answer and some obstacle put in the way can be the solution. A couple of chairs put on the bed will make sure that there is no room for the dog. However, if the bedroom door is kept shut no other precautions are necessary. A dining room chair placed upside down on the fireside chair will prevent its occupation during your absence. The same solution with two chairs will invalidate the settee.

The balloon technique discussed in Problem 5.7 can be an alternative. Balloons placed on the bed or chair will ensure that these pieces of furniture will be given a wide berth.

Aggressively possessive dogs can be prevented from getting on to furniture by the means described, but getting them off when already established is another matter. This is discussed under Problem 8.2.

The remedies discussed can take time to become effective. It is a case of cultivating new alternative canine habits, such as training the dog to sleep in his own bed or on the floor until the memory of chair comfort has gone from his mind.

Preventive Measures You Can Take

These measures are based on ensuring that the floor and his bed are the correct places for your dog. Even as a puppy he should not be picked up or allowed to climb on to your lap while you are sitting. Some dogs will not connect being picked up with the comfort of a fireside chair, but many others will.

Problem 5.9 – BARKING DOGS

My dog is the most persistent barker. Anybody passing the house sets him off. The excitement of getting ready to take him for a walk can cause such a noise, and it is impossible to make him stop until we get out on to the street.

An Understanding and Probable Causes

Barking is a very natural outlet for a dog who wishes to express himself. Some dogs will bark at the least excuse or provocation, while others are so inhibited that they find no reason to make such a noise. Some breeds are more likely to bark than others: terriers seem to find more reason to bark than most other breeds, but even within a breed or a single litter of puppies there can be wide variations in barking thresholds.

The environment in which a puppy is brought up can have quite an influence on a dog's natural capacity for barking. Excitable children in one home can create a strong and abundant capacity for canine vocal expression, yet in a home with an older dog the younger one may never show signs of such vocal content. This can be for one of two reasons: the older dog barks when necessary and the younger dog is happy to let the older and more dominant dog do all the work and protecting necessary. On the other hand, the older dog's barking can be controlled by the owner telling him to 'shut up' and the younger dog learns that the older dog's barking creates an unpleasant reaction from the owner and becomes inhibited to the degree that extenuating circumstances are required to raise any vocal response from that youngster.

Barking due to the stress or distress of being left alone is covered by Problem 5.5 and this should be fully studied. Dogs also bark as an indication of their aggressive attitude: aggressive tendencies are covered in Chapter Eight.

Many owners encourage barking to create a deterrent against possible criminal activities and then find that they cannot control the situation.

Barking is a sign of dominance, the dog is either dominating or trying to dominate the situation. He is barking *at* something or *for* something. He can be barking at an intruder, another dog or a cat in the garden. He can be barking for attention, his meal or through impatience because you have given the signals which tell him it is exercise time. Whatever the cause of barking – the *at* or *for* situation – the source should be recognised and the events anticipated. If an owner knows when to expect barking he can be more prepared to prevent or stop it before the dog has reached an insensitive high, when it may require a much more demanding approach to achieve a responsible canine attitude.

REMEDIAL ACTION YOU CAN TAKE

It must first be recognised that unless you or a colleague are present to take effective action you will not be able to stop your dog from barking, although at any time you may be able to take avoiding action which takes away the cause or reason for barking.

As Problem 5.5 deals with dogs that do not wish to be left alone and includes dogs that bark for this reason, nothing further is required in this section.

There are many instances of barking which just require the application of control. The basic training already discussed in Chapter Two will ensure that you get and maintain your dog's attention under normal conditions and it also forms the basis for achieving success under more demanding conditions.

On many occasions barking is a form of defiance which can be interpreted as a product of aggression and can be countered by using a more penetrating bark (noise) than the dog to show your own aggressive nature with a vocal response. A period of longer than three seconds for your own vocal response to take effect indicates that the strength of your countering action is insufficient and other approaches will initially be required before reverting to the purely vocal countering measures.

Let us consider the arrival of the postman, milkman or some other visitor as being the cause of excited barking either as a welcome or an aggressive warning. The use of the six foot cord is most appropriate and this can be attached to the dog's collar so that he can trail it behind him.

With the first sign of agitated activity get hold of the end of the cord and tug as necessary, as you call your dog's name. Immediately move backwards into the attention-getting routine. Keep his attention on yourself and away from the cause of the disruption by vocal and physical inducements. On achieving success give praise and a reward, if available, then move forward towards the cause and try to maintain full attentiveness. With any resumption of agitation or barking repeat the attention-getting backward movement. If necessary, make your dog sit and create a more inhibiting atmosphere.

There are other methods which may well be effective in shaking a dominant dog out of uncontrolled barking. The banging of two baking tins right behind him may bring him into a more responsible attitude. A squirt of clean water from a squeezy bottle can be quite effective or the use of a mugger/rape alarm can achieve sensibility. One such alarm which is produced as an aerosol with a high pitched screech is marketed principally for canine control and is called the *Dog Stop*. This item has been introduced by Dr Roger Mugford and can probably be obtained through your own vet.

Any method which is used to gain the dog's attention under these circumstances is likely to be unpleasant and its successful application should be followed by pleasantness and praise.

You may well wish to control barking but still have your dog give voice when somebody comes to the door so that you have maintained the deterrent aspect of your dog's presence. Under these circumstances the above applies, but each time your dog starts barking because of outside activity give him praise and encouragement for some five seconds of uninhibited vocal reaction before you demand a quiet, controlled situation.

A dog who gets excited and barks incessantly when you are preparing to take him out for a walk should be curbed at the first bark and inhibited by one of the methods already discussed until you are ready to put the lead on and open the door.

PREVENTIVE MEASURES YOU CAN TAKE

Preventive measures can be based on maintaining a less excited situation, especially when it is likely to result in barking. If excited children in the family start a dog barking – control the children. If routine visitations from the postman, milkman, paper girl or someone else is going to create a reaction – keep the dog in another part of the house during these timed visits.

It can be difficult or impossible to prevent a dog from deciding he it going to bark and I doubt if it is wise to try and completely eliminate such a natural canine expression. It is probably more in keeping to try to restrain a dog's vocal contribution. The earlier this feature of a dog's upbringing is controlled the easier it is to achieve a balanced situation.

Problem 5.10 – INDOOR KENNELLING

Because my young puppy was so destructive while left on his own I was advised to get an indoor kennel for him. However, he does not like this form of restriction and makes quite a noise when he is put into the kennel when we have to go out.

AN UNDERSTANDING AND PROBABLE CAUSES

The type of indoor kennel being used can affect a dog's ability to settle and accept restrictions. The introduction to such restrictions, the timing of them and the activity within sight or sound of the dog can also have an effect on his acquiescence to the prevailing conditions.

A child's play-pen supplemented with fine chicken wire may be used as an indoor kennel, especially for small dogs who cannot jump out. A wooden erection which blocks a dog's view can also be classed as an indoor kennel. Some very small dogs are confined to purpose-built carrying boxes with a grill front, the type which are commonly seen at dog shows. However, the most common style in use is a purpose-built pen (or cage) and these vary in size to suit most breeds of dog.

Any indoor kennel should be large enough for the purpose intended and the likely duration of habitation. If a puppy or dog requires a toilet area this area should be large enough to accommodate both toilet and sleeping requirements. Space for a water dish and possibly a feeding bowl must also be considered. In fact it should be a home from home with all the necessary comforts and not just a convenient place to stick the dog out of harm's way. The dog should be comfortable and feel at ease, or if the accommodation is being set up for a puppy, his growth should be considered. Allow for his full size as an adult of the breed.

Problems can result from failing to provide a satisfactory introduction period, and causing stress instead of creating an assured relaxed atmosphere. Children playing in the area or the presence of other animals flouting their freedom are likely to provoke a distraught captive animal.

Remedial and Preventive Action You Can Take

Dogs who have an objection to indoor kennels can be treated in the same way as puppies being conditioned to accept contented confinement (Problem 5.5). However, barriers will have to be broken down and stress built up during periods of penned discontentment must be overcome and negated.

A gradual introduction is the answer. Feeding in or beside the indoor kennel and in your presence is a starting point. Bedding which has been used and is well scented by the dog should be placed inside. During the quiet of the evening when the dog usually has a sleep he can be put inside while you sit beside him. As most indoor kennels are moveable it can be placed by your fireside chair. When your dog is accustomed to this type of situation he can be put into the indoor kennel initially at feeding times and sleeping times only. If necessary the kennel can be moved to the kitchen or into the garden if you are working outside. Isolation should be considered only when the dog is completely relaxed and accepts the indoor kennel as a place of refuge. He should be able to go into it of his own accord at any time he wishes.

Initially periods of deliberate isolation should be short and your dog should not be let out when he demands it; only let him out when he is calm and composed. Otherwise your dog will learn to demand his release by barking or whining. If you have left him too long and he is upset, ignore him but sit beside the kennel and relax until he has calmed down, then you can let him out. An indoor kennel should not be abused by utilising it as a convenient means of putting a dog unnecessarily out of the way. When used with consideration a dog can be quite contented with his protected sleeping quarters.

CHAPTER SIX

Lead Walking Problems

One just has to watch the normal morning or evening dog walks to the local park or favourite exercise area to see the antics of the various dogs: a Toy Poodle who pulls at the end of a fine show lead but it appears to be no concern to the owner; an Irish Setter who is scared of heavy vehicles which pass with thundering madness; a Jack Russell Terrier who darts back and forth in front of the owner like an accident looking for somewhere to happen; an overfed Golden Retriever who is following the owner at a snail's pace; a Cocker Spaniel who finds an interesting sniff at every lamppost and gateway; or a Cairn Terrier who will snap at every other dog he passes.

Although particular breeds are mentioned they could be any of a number of other breeds – yours could be one of them. The problems are there to be viewed by anybody who cares to look. However, some of the owners will not see them as problems – perhaps the owner of the Toy Poodle does not mind being pulled along, although it would be a different story if the dog was a Rottweiler. The overfed Golden Retriever may have an owner in the same condition who is quite happy to walk at that pace with his dog trailing behind. There is only a problem when the owner realises that the dog is not reacting on the lead to his own requirements or if the difficulties are affecting any other members of the public.

Although many dog owners can walk their dogs without problems all owners should find something of value in this chapter. One notable omission is that of aggressive dogs, this is dealt with in Chapter Eight.

Problem 6.1 – PULLING ON THE LEAD

My dog continually pulls while on the lead when out for a walk. He pulls to the extent of appearing to choke himself.

AN UNDERSTANDING AND PROBABLE CAUSES

This problem has a number of variations. Some dogs will pull on the lead constantly while others pull only part of the time. The dog might pull through excitement when going out for a walk, but then walk nicely on the way home after a good romp. Others may pull on the way home because it is getting very near to feeding time. Some will pull to get to another dog – as a friend or a foe. Some dogs will continually get under the owner's feet by crossing directly in front of them and others will stop and sniff at anything that takes their fancy.

As already mentioned in Chapter Three the practice of pulling on the lead is normally allowed to develop from the first day a puppy is taken out for a walk when it causes no discomfort for the owner to be pulled along by a youngster. However, maturity brings strength along with canine leadership to the fore. The practice of pulling on the lead has been allowed to develop to the degree that it will be difficult to stop.

Unfortunately, when most people take the dog out for a walk it is time for mental relaxation, time to let the mind wander, or perhaps time to think about a family or business problem. The dog is far from being relaxed and is eager to enjoy his outing. He is usually given little attention until the arm aches or a sudden change in direction causes the owner to fall over his dog or be confronted with some other problem because of a major distraction which could have been noted and countered by a more alert mind.

REMEDIAL ACTION YOU CAN TAKE

The attention-getting training routine described in Chapter Two up to the third target is the basis for good loose lead walking. The attention-getting routine should be continued until the dog's attention can be maintained as a training routine for some thirty seconds or so. This training routine is not only the foundation for loose lead walking but it is also a foundation which is essential if success is to be achieved within other areas. The return to such a training routine may well be required from time to time to sharpen a dog's attentive outlook.

While out walking it is very important that the dog is not allowed at any time to become the leader by forging ahead or by deviating in the direction of some interesting distraction. Any such movement on the dog's part should be countered immediately by the backward attention-getting movement described in Chapter Two.

The forward walking movement with your dog at your left side is a requirement for attention getting, but it is also the principal requirement for loose lead walking where the spells of forward movement can be gradually extended in training. Walks on the lead should initially be kept as short as possible to ensure that you can apply the training approach during the walk. If it is handy to take the dog in the car nearer to the exercise area, short lead walks and free exercise will be of greater value than a long walk with continual correction.

You should also be sufficiently observant to anticipate undesirable actions from your dog and be prepared to prevent these actions from taking place. Quite often a word of warning to the dog is sufficient, but at other times sudden backward movement should be made immediately prior to the anticipated undesirable canine action.

With some very strong-willed dogs, especially of the larger breeds, and particularly for owners of these dogs who do not have matching physical statures, the only realistic answer may be the use of the halti to obtain a suitable and acceptable loose lead walking situation.

A dog generally requires a little time to become accustomed to the halti and the instructions with the product should be observed.

Once the dog is accustomed to this form of control the training discussed in the context of this problem can be applied.

There are other activities which can help to keep a dog generally in line with your body while out lead walking. The waving of an object such as a light branch of a tree with a few leaves on the end or a walking stick in front of the dog's face can help to keep him in line. Alternatively the walking stick can be held by the bottom end with the hooked handle being used to catch in the hind leg of the dog when he starts to move ahead of you. This can make him very watchful for a repeat and may therefore make him stay in line with you. Some dogs find this practice to be too disagreeable and it can create more problems than it resolves. Discretion should be applied.

Another technique is pinching the loose skin at the dog's groin. As the dog, while walking at your left side, moves forward ahead of you, catch the dog's groin at his right side with your left hand and give it a smart nip. This is a very tender area for most dogs and in future the movement of your hand with intent can keep your dog in line. If the dog has aggressive tendencies and is likely to bite you when applying this technique, control over the aggression must be achieved before using this corrective measure.

The flexi-lead can be used to good purpose in the latter stages of training for loose lead walking. However, its popular application with the majority of dog owners who use the flexi-lead does encourage canine leadership and, therefore, pulling on the lead. It is strongly recommended that the flexi-lead be used principally when limited freedom is being given at some exercise area. When used in the latter stages of training the flexi-lead can be introduced on completion of the third target of the attention-getting training routine to assess the control being achieved without the need to apply the stop control button. The flexi-lead is of greater value when training a dog to come back when called and this is brought out in the appropriate section.

Kerb drill is a very useful addition to lead control. Always halt at the kerb before crossing a road and make the dog stay at your side on a loose lead for some three to five seconds at least before thinking of crossing the road. The dog can be made to sit if you wish but it is not essential. To stand and wait is sufficient but be consistent. If you want the dog to sit then make sure he does it.

The attention-getting training routine for the fourth to sixth targets covers the instant sit when required for kerb drill or it can be utilised to prevent lead pulling. This is especially useful with an excited dog wanting to get out for a walk. He can be made to sit to have the lead put on and to sit again while the door or gate is being opened. He can also be made to wait sitting or to remain standing behind you until you have gone through the doorway or gate.

An excited dog should be taught to give right of way to the owner. During a walk changes in preventive or corrective action can be applied to maintain or regain a loose lead situation. On some occasions a halt and sit can be applied to prevent lead pulling and on other occasions the backward movement can be applied. The walking stick or the light branch of a tree can be utilised and on occasion the nip in the groin can effectively surprise him. However, anticipation and a warning word or two with good timing to prevent the effect of a distraction can often be the most successful way of consolidating the training programme.

When lead walking with your dog, it is important to recognise that a dog is likely to dictate the walking speed if you train or try to condition his responses by walking at the speed which suits him. For instance, if he wants to go fast and you try to control at that speed, he will soon learn to govern the speed. If he wants to walk fast you should slow down a bit and make him walk on a loose lead at the pace you set. If he wants to walk slower than your normal speed you should walk faster and entice your dog to maintain the correct position beside you.

Preventive Measures You Can Take

The prevention strategy starts before a puppy is taken for his first walk, but the same tactics can also be adopted with more mature puppies or older dogs who have already chosen to become leaders. The prevention strategy can be applied in conjunction with the remedial activities already discussed.

The equipment initially required is a six foot length of line with a clip attached as recommended in Chapter One, along with a traditional collar or combi-collar. A check chain is not recommended at this stage.

Initially let the puppy get accustomed to dragging the cord around the house while supervised. As there are no knots or loops to catch under doors or elsewhere, the only time the puppy feels a 'check' is when you intentionally step on or pick up the end of the line.

Each time a 'check' is carried out get down to the puppy's level, call his name and encourage him to come back to you. Carry out this form of 'check' from time to time until the puppy automatically comes back without the need to call his name.

While he is on the short line do not let the puppy go from one room to another ahead of you. If he is ahead, step on and pick up the end of the line, call him back and let him proceed at your left side on the loose line or behind you as you go through the doorway. Any attempt to move ahead should be stopped with a short sharp tug and application of the backward movement to achieve instant attention, or you can make him sit for a few seconds to regain a more respectful attitude.

Remember that every unpleasant act on your part, no matter how small, should be followed by signs of appreciation as soon as you gain the puppy's attention and a desirable result.

If you have a garden the process can be extended to that area to get the puppy accustomed to a change of environment. When taking the puppy out for his first walk the lead can be used or a temporary holding loop can be tied at the end of the line. The first venture out of the front door and garden gate should be the time to keep the puppy's attention on yourself with encouragement as required. If necessary make your puppy sit for a few seconds before going through the door or gate. This will help to ensure that your puppy does not move ahead of you.

The foundation has now been laid for a controlled puppy walk. Distractions which influence the puppy will occur and these early opportunities to maintain control should not be missed. A little sharp tug on the lead should be sufficient but, if not, the backward movement or an enforced sit should come into operation. If the distraction is one which is friendly based, such as meeting a friend or a known friendly dog where a measure of fraternising is acceptable to you, then your restriction on the puppy can be lifted with a positive 'O.K. you can welcome him now'.

Although this section has concentrated on puppy lead training, it is repeated that the procedure and the remedial action can be applied to more adult dogs who already create related lead walking problems.

Whatever training is given to counter or prevent lead pulling, until consistently good responses are achieved, the results can be nullified by a relaxed and inattentive owner approach when out walking. Even with good results the passage of time can create the need for a short programme of retraining to maintain a satisfactory performance.

THE ACCEPTABLE SITUATION

This depends entirely on what is considered to be acceptable to the individual owner. Ideally, when out walking, the dog should walk nicely at the owner's left side and be sufficiently observant to maintain that position when the owner has changed direction or has stopped.

Some dogs will take advantage of any excess loose lead and walk ahead of the owner; they do not actually pull but they take advantage of every inch of lead available. To many people this is acceptable although it would be advisable to limit the length of lead available.

Although Chapter Two on training describes a method for holding and using the lead, this is principally a technique for training or correcting the dog who has lapsed into the old habit.

A very convenient method of holding the lead is to slip the end of the loop over three fingers of the left hand and then hold the lead at the appropriate distance from the collar between the thumb and index finger. This is the point of control, the excess lead drops in a long loop at your left side and is available for use as required.

It is important that whatever you consider to be acceptable should be consistently applied. A dog cannot understand why he is allowed to pull on the lead one day but not the next.

Problem 6.2 – LAGGING ON THE LEAD

My dog tends to lag behind me when we go out for a walk, particularly on our way out. On the way home from our walk he does not lag so much.

An Understanding and Probable Causes

The variations in this type of problem have to be examined to ascertain the actual cause. Some dogs find no pleasure in going for a walk but appreciate when they are on the way home. Other dogs find a particular point of a regular walk to be uncomfortable and can lag badly in that area, something unpleasant has happened to cause the dog's concern.

The probable cause of the case in question is likely to go back to the dog's introduction to walking on the lead as a puppy. A puppy or young dog goes out for its first walk – or it could be a more mature dog that has just changed ownership and does not want to go – the owner pulls the dog along and possibly creates panic in the dog's mind. Eventually the dog goes because he has no option but he is miserable and very uncertain of his owner under these circumstances. No wonder the dog does not want to walk beside him. If he is a young puppy, his mind can be scarred for life and he may never be happy on the lead.

Unfortunately this practice of just walking on and pulling the dog behind is recommended by a number of behaviourists and trainers. It may work perfectly well for some dogs, particularly in the hands of an expert, but a number of dogs never seem to get over the experience.

Lagging also can be due to canine ill health, arthritic or other physical ailments which can cause the dog some distress. Sometimes we just do not appreciate a dog's health or even temporary physical problems. Lagging could be a learned habit after having such an ailment: the dog has learned through sympathy to enjoy a slow relaxed walk.

The owner may have made his dog so subdued and inhibited by his own overbearing attitude that the dog has fully accepted his place in the pecking order, at the back of the line, and he feels that this is where he should walk. Some owners are so quiet and inhibited themselves that they have infected their dogs with the same inhibitions.

We must not forget the mismatched dog and owner: for example, a small Yorkshire Terrier being walked by a six foot tall man of athletic stature who is accustomed to striding out smartly. The little fellow just does not have a chance of keeping up with him.

Remedial Action You Can Take

The attention-getting training routine described in Chapter Two up to the third target is strongly recommended as a starting point. However, during this period of training it is extremely important that the full routine be carried out with excitement, encouragement, rewards and praise.

Initially some 80 per cent of your movement should be backwards, thus encouraging the dog to follow at an energetic pace. Very gradually your backward movement can be reduced to 20 per cent of the time with the dog happily walking by your side. Much of your forward movement can be carried out at faster than a smart walking pace.

During this training period try to avoid walking situations where the dog is likely to lag. If necessary take the dog out in the car to his exercise area, give him some fun and games, put him on the lead for a short walk and use the attention-getting routine as necessary if there is any sign of lagging. Do not be frightened to use encouragement with great enthusiasm during parts of this walking time or even all of the time if it is necessary. After the period of lead walking give the dog more off-lead fun and games before coming home in the car.

When you feel that the training is achieving good results go out for your normal walk and whenever a lagging situation is likely to recur, immediately counter it by applying your backward movement, but in the direction you intend walking. Use enthusiasm, encouragement, reward (titbits) and praise as you achieve a greater speed than normal. After some fifteen to twenty paces resume your normal walking stature but apply encouragement as required.

When a dog slows down always create a greater than normal speed to achieve greater excitement and momentum. If you slow down to the dog's pace he will go even slower.

Unpleasantness under certain conditions can cause a dog to lag whilst in that particular area only. A dog can be upset by exhaust fumes from a bus or lorry, especially if he crosses the road behind such a vehicle. After such an incident he may lag or shy away from any similar vehicle he is expected to pass. He may have been hit by a bicycle at some time and its presence can have the same effect.

An aggressive dog behind a garden gate can give many a dog a fright and cause extreme apprehension every time an affected dog passes the gate. Each such situation creates a sense of insecurity.

In each of these circumstances, and in others of a similar nature, it is important that the dog's mind is taken off the past event when that particular area is being passed or when the circumstances of the moment are going to affect the dog's sense of insecurity.

To give him sympathy is fatal and this will only make the dog believe that he has reason to feel insecure. Attention getting with enthusiastic encouragement to stay with you is the real answer. Praise and reward will help to take his attention away from the imaginary situation. Your own backward movement at a good pace to maintain attention may be necessary for some time until the dog realises that no further harm will come to him in that situation.

PREVENTIVE MEASURES YOU CAN TAKE

The preventive measures described in Problem 6.1 are applicable in this case and the conditioning with a collar and six foot line would be most appropriate.

If a puppy is of a shy and retiring nature, greater encouragement with generous praise and reward are required to overcome unwillingness to mix with the outside world. Sympathy will only hinder your progress. Utilise the preventive measures in Problem 6.1 to the full but apply corrective measures which involve unpleasantness with the greatest caution.

Problem 6.3 – SNIFFING ON THE LEAD

When out walking with my dog on the lead he stops and sniffs at every excuse: it can be a tuft of grass, a tree, a gate-post or a lamppost, he is not fussy. He seems to be so easily distracted by any smell which takes his interest. He also seems to lift his leg on many of these occasions (urinating).

AN UNDERSTANDING AND PROBABLE CAUSES

With a great number of dogs this canine practice of stopping and sniffing is just a habit which has been allowed to develop. It is the male dog who generally shows the greatest inclination to stop and sniff and he is, of course, the leg lifter. By urinating in these specific areas, which are already contaminated with scents left by other dogs, your dog is marking his own areas, i.e. territorial marking. This may be due to a degree of dominance in your dog, he may be highly sexed or it can be more in line with habit. However, the causes are generally connected.

Whatever the reasons we give for the practice or habit, the dog has been allowed to control events. If he wants to stop and investigate he will do it and many owners do not seem to appreciate that it is weakness on their part which has allowed the practice to develop and continue.

The basic problem may also be due to a recall problem. Many owners who cannot get their dogs to come back when called after a spell of freedom do not let their dogs off the lead. As the dog never has freedom to choose a specific location within an exercise area for his toilet requirements, he is unconsciously being encouraged by the owner to stop and investigate attractive smells at every opportunity.

REMEDIAL ACTION YOU CAN TAKE

It is important that your dog is given the opportunity to relieve himself when he feels the need, but the time and place is not while he is out walking on the lead.

Your dog can be walked on the lead directly to an exercise area and then given the opportunity to relieve himself. He can be given freedom off the lead, at the end of a flexi-lead or a long line or, if there is no other choice available, on the lead. He may be given opportunities to perform at other exercise areas during a walk or just before returning home, but he must learn to know the difference between a permitted area where he is allowed to sniff around for the spot which suits him and being walked on the lead.

The basic training requirements which cover both pulling on the lead and lagging on the lead may well be required as a foundation for your remedial action. They should be studied and practised to ensure that you have mastered the techniques and your dog has the experience to respond.

The habit of stopping to sniff or urinate at will is best tackled by observing when and where your dog is likely to stop and, therefore, being prepared for the event before it actually happens.

Inviting lampposts, gate-posts and the like are already known to you. As you approach one, and at the moment you expect your dog to take an interest, use his name with urgency and meaning to maintain his attention until you have passed the distraction. Then give him praise and a reward if desired for being so attentive.

You may on occasion, or if your dog is very strong willed, continue in your intended direction but turn round and move backwards drawing your dog with you by means of an urgent attention-getting attitude. A single short tug may be required but otherwise a loose lead must be maintained. He should not be pulled along at the end of a tight lead.

On other occasions you may be taken by surprise (due to your own inattention) and your dog stops to sniff. You should immediately move backwards, in the direction you have just walked and into an attention-getting routine. On achieving your objective – his undivided attention – change direction again and with your dog in the loose lead walking position walk past the interesting distraction. During this period keep his attention on yourself: you may warn him 'DON'T YOU DARE' as you are approaching the obstacle. Again praise and reward your dog for his cooperation.

PREVENTIVE MEASURES YOU CAN TAKE

You can start by taking avoiding measures to remove the temptation of interesting lampposts and gate-posts. This can be done by walking on the inside or outside edge of the pavement to put yourself between the interesting distraction and your dog.

Use of exercise areas is also very important and if possible dogs should be off the lead during the periods when they are being encouraged (by association) to relieve themselves. While browsing during these periods a bit of sniffing and territorial marking does not normally cause problems and this applies to both canine sexes. It normally helps to satisfy instinctive needs.

While your dog is on the lead and walking by your side you should *never* give him the opportunity to sniff the ground or at any object which could arouse territorial marking instincts. Puppies brought up in this manner are never a problem.

Problem 6.4 – LEAD WALKING AND TRAFFIC

My dog cannot get accustomed to traffic when we are out for a walk. He seems to be worse when he hears the air brakes of a heavy truck.

AN UNDERSTANDING AND PROBABLE CAUSES

A number of dogs seem to lack confidence when traffic is around and in this day and age it is difficult to walk along any road or street without meeting traffic.

Dogs who have not been introduced to traffic as youngsters can be very apprehensive. Also any young puppies who are forced to take their first walk down a road with heavy or continuous traffic may show this apprehension for the rest of their lives, particularly if the sudden noise of air brakes on a heavy truck occurred during a period when the youngster was full of uncertainty.

Some dogs are only worried about traffic during the hours of darkness. Again this may be due to the introduction as a puppy to a traffic situation or it may be due to an unpleasant occurrence during darkness when he feels that the lights of a vehicle approaching are a sign of danger.

I can recall the situation with my first German Shepherd Dog over thirty years ago. He would move away from the edge of the pavement when a heavy truck passed; to this day, I do not know the cause of the problem. It may be because he was brought up in a quiet residential area or that during his introduction to heavy traffic an exhaust or air brakes upset him. He was very stable and dependable at all other times; he could even stand close to a level crossing when an express train passed at high speed without acknowledging its presence. He travelled on London tube trains from time to time and the rush of a train coming into the station had no effect on him. However, when a heavy truck passed he edged away until it had gone. If we had had today's knowledge at that time we might have appreciated the original cause and could have taken steps to remove this uncertainty in his mind.

With some dogs uncertainty in traffic may be an understatement.

The dog may be absolutely scared of any traffic. The dog's introduction to traffic or a single happening, such as an accident, may have created the dog's complete rejection of all traffic or just the general type of vehicle which caused such an impression on his mind.

A dog of strong character may in time get over the unpleasant circumstances which caused his reaction to traffic, particularly when an owner has a considerate and constructive attitude. However, a dog who lacks this strength of character may require expert help to overcome his fear of traffic; even with this help he may not respond fully to the applied therapy.

REMEDIAL ACTION YOU CAN TAKE

It is essential that the effect of passing traffic be minimised, so that your dog is not subjected to the trauma of traffic passing too close to him until favourable conditioning has had the opportunity to become fully effective.

There are a number of avoiding actions which should be given serious consideration:

1. If possible avoid streets where the type of traffic which is causing concern is likely to pass.
2. When passing traffic is inevitable walk at the inside of the left pavement. As your dog is at your left side he is walking as far away as practical from the traffic and your body will act as a shield. It may be that your dog is more concerned about traffic coming up behind him than coming towards him. If this is the case walk facing the oncoming traffic, but, if possible, keep your dog at your left side. To change your dog to your right side may cause confusion unless you always wish to have him walk at your right side. This will also cause confusion in your mind if you need to carry out any of the training procedures.
3. Avoid crossing a busy road if possible. Standing at the edge of the pavement waiting for a break in the traffic can create a greater trauma than any other lead walking situation.

Positive conditioning should now be considered and this can be varied according to the availability of suitable areas for training.

Try to find a play area close to a busy road and with a wire mesh fence separating the play area from the road. If it is only possible to find a play area which is open to the road, a flexi-lead or dragging line will probably have to be used to eliminate the possibility of an accident.

The basic objective is for your dog to enjoy himself and be more interested in you or play toys than in any passing traffic. This enjoyment should commence at a distance from the road where the traffic will cause absolutely no concern to your dog.

At times some attention getting on the lead can be applied with rewards and fun. Toys or sticks can also be thrown for him. It may be advisable to refrain from using a ball because it might roll on to the road. This fun can be carried out freely, on a flexi-lead or on a long line as the facilities and reactions dictate.

During each conditioning session move a little nearer to the road but watch for any sign of an unsatisfactory reaction from your dog. If there is a wire mesh fence between the play area and the road you can try throwing the play toy towards the road, but start throwing in that direction when the traffic is light. If the dog reacts you have gone too close to the road before he is ready for it. Do not sympathise with him; laugh and joke, tell him not to be silly, and run away with excitement to get his full attention back on to yourself.

When lead walking on the pavement watch for his reactions and as they improve move into the centre of the pavement. Build up confidence and when you see or hear a vehicle approaching which is likely to cause your dog concern, get his attention on yourself before it passes. Use titbits and excitement to maintain his attention until the vehicle is safely past.

With dogs that show apprehension towards traffic during the hours of darkness unpleasant situations should be avoided until suitable conditioning has been carried out. Walking in traffic should occur just before the light begins to go, with the return home timed to coincide with the failing light. The timing of a walk can be slightly modified until darkness has descended on the road home.

The gradual process of conditioning and building confidence is again important and your reaction to possible situations caused by passing traffic at night is the same as given for daytime traffic problems.

The preventive measures given in Problem 6.1 apply fully to the prevention of traffic problems. Remember that your dog should feel completely at ease on the lead and street lead walking should be introduced in a quiet atmosphere during the gradual introduction to traffic situations.

Although dogs should not be sheltered from the realities of life they should not be pushed into situations they cannot handle.

Problem 6.5 – SNAPPING AT PEOPLE PASSING

I have a young dog from one of the guarding breeds and while I am out walking him on the lead he has a tendency to have a little nip at people passing by. It does not appear to be motivated by aggression but rather by a desire to get people's attention. This is very worrying and as some people move their arm away with a sharp movement I am concerned that he may bite somebody.

AN UNDERSTANDING AND PROBABLE CAUSES

This problem does come to the fore from time to time and usually occurs with youngsters when they go through their period of adolescence. This seems to be a period of uncertainty in their lives when it would appear that some dogs wish to protect their owners. With others nipping seems to be a means of gaining the attention of a passer-by. It is a case of 'Speak to me, I want to be friends'. The fact that some people jerk the arm away when this happens can actually encourage the dog to bite. However, people cannot be blamed for taking this evasive action. Whatever the reason, it can be rather disconcerting for people when passing such dogs in the street.

This problem can often disappear as the youngster develops and gains greater confidence. He no longer finds it necessary to show this form of protection or to seek friends in this manner. However, with other youngsters it may be the start of a more aggressive canine attitude.

An owner cannot afford to wait and find out which way nature and environmental conditions are going to affect a youngster's future actions and he must act to eliminate the problem at its onset.

REMEDIAL ACTION YOU CAN TAKE

The attention-getting training routine as described in Chapter Two up to the third target is strongly recommended as a starting point.

The routines should be studied and practised to ensure that you have mastered the techniques and your dog has the experience to respond. You should also have the ability and foresight to get and keep your dog's attention when you suspect that he is going to take notice of some innocent passer-by.

If you cannot, have the person pass on your right side or try to avoid passing too close to the person if your dog is going to be between the two of you when passing. Any form of diversion will do so long as you can get his attention on yourself as you are about to pass the other party.

Create excitement and move away from the person if he is passing next to your dog. A side-step to your right at the correct moment as you get his attention may be quite sufficient. As an alternative measure a backward movement to make your dog turn to follow you, again at the correct moment, can also be very effective. Have your dog wondering what you are going to do at the moment he is thinking about the passer-by.

Always give a reward and use excited praise the moment you have achieved your objective – that is when it is too late for your dog to act against the person passing by.

PREVENTIVE MEASURES YOU CAN TAKE

There are no real preventive measures you can take but you can be observant for the first indication of nipping and then introduce the remedies described. If you feel that the problem is aggression-based it would be advisable to study Chapter Eight concerning aggression.

CHAPTER SEVEN

Off-lead Problems

So many problems come to the fore when a dog becomes detached from his lead. With an open space to run free, be it in a park, on the beach, on common ground or in open country, there are many distractions which seem to result in complete and utter canine deafness to the urgent calls of his owner. Some dogs will come back in their own good time, while others refuse to come back and will keep out of the owner's reach or disappear for many hours and then return home when they are hungry or in need of a warm bed for the night.

To many owners there seems to be no consistency in their dogs' response to the call to come back. Some owners say, 'He can be so disobedient when there are children playing'. Others say, 'He just ignores me when there is another dog around'. Still others say, 'He comes back most times when called', but further investigation indicates that the response is completely negative when there is any distraction which takes his attention.

Although owners must accept full responsibility for allowing most of these situations to develop, it is understandable as there is a lack of education to ensure that owners appreciate the significance of giving dogs uncontrolled freedom before influential training has been carried out.

Some breeds of dog are more easily controlled than others. Many dogs do not like to be away from their owners, while others can become very independent. Irish Setters have a reputation for enjoying uncontrolled freedom and members of the Gaze Hound breeds can forget that they belong to anybody when liberty presents itself. Let a Beagle get the scent of a hare while out in the country and he can become oblivious to anything else until he has run out of track; he may come home or just go looking for the scent path of another hare.

The age of a dog can also have an effect on his desire for freedom to play with other dogs or children. Puppies who initially have come back when called may develop a desire for a more independent approach to life as they go through adolescence. If the first signs are not appreciated the foundation of a problem may be laid.

Whatever the breed or age of the dog, uncontrolled freedom with the inability to regain control is probably the most widespread and worrying problem in dog ownership. There is no doubt that the following factors must be observed and put into full operation to avert such uncontrolled situations:

1. Specific training to achieve control.
2. Observation and anticipation to prevent uncontrolled situations from developing.
3. Avoidance procedures – changing freedom areas or times to avoid expected problems and also maintaining lead control until the possible problem situation has been averted.

When a dog has experienced uncontrolled freedom and realises that defiance results in continued liberty, time and hard work on the part of the owner will be required to regain full control.

Although various situations will be described in this chapter each problem is strongly related to Problem 7. 1 and the basic training discussed under that problem should also be carried out.

Problem 7.1 – DOGS WHO WILL NOT COME BACK WHEN CALLED

As a puppy my young dog was quite obedient when out and off the lead. He never went more than about thirty paces away and always came back to me when called. He is now a year old and he seems to have developed a mind of his own. As soon as he is let off the lead he goes sniffing all over the place and the sight of another dog takes him away to play. He ignores my call to come back and when he eventually does respond he runs round me and I cannot catch him.

An Understanding and Probable Causes

Dogs will usually come back to their owners when called if there is no good reason for staying away. Any comprehension of this problem is based on this premise, but why do dogs stay away?

A never-ending list of reasons can be given for dogs staying away when called, but each reason comes down to four basic and variable causes which may also interact with each other to indicate an inconsistency on the part of the dog. The four basic causes are:

1. Strength of distraction.
2. Canine apprehension.
3. Owner control.
4. Owner attentiveness.

1. Strength of distraction
A distraction is anything which takes a dog's interest; for instance, an enticing smell can make a dog oblivious to all the shouts and threats from an owner. Children playing in the park can mean sheer joy to a playful dog and I have seen a cricket match being temporarily stopped after a six hit when a Retriever enjoyed being chased all over the place by the players wanting to regain possession of the cricket ball. Meeting with a playful canine companion can also create two distraught and irate owners.

2. Canine apprehension
At this juncture it is important that Chapter One, Understanding Your Dog, is fully appreciated, in particular the section relating to canine logic. Many dogs are punished because they do not come back to their owners when called. This punishment may only be verbal abuse or it may be a more physical response from the owner. If a temper has been lost then the punishment can be extremely severe.

It should now be remembered that a dog recognises a pleasant or unpleasant situation will result from the act he is performing or has just performed. To receive punishment the dog must be with the owner; he is therefore receiving very unpleasant treatment for coming back and not for staying away. With this in a dog's mind, the next time he is called in he will not be happy about receiving another unpleasant reception. Two or three repetitions of this pattern will ensure that the dog prefers to stay away in the hope that his owner will be more receptive in time.

3. Owner control

Control is based on training and an understanding between dog and owner, although it should be noted that quite a number of owners do not need to apply a formal training programme to achieve the desired control. Some dogs and owners seem to be very well matched and to have a great deal of understanding of each other. These owners can also visualise difficulties before they arise and can take avoiding action. A loose dog arrives on the scene and the owner calls his own dog in before there is an opportunity for them to mix. The owner knows the extent of his control but he may or may not know what to expect from the other dog and his owner, so he does not wait until it is too late for preventive action. Owners never have full 100 per cent control under all possible situations while the dog is off the lead but they should be able to control or prevent most undesirable situations from developing. All too often owners are affected by the actions of others. One example of such a situation follows.

An owner of two very well-trained German Shepherd Dogs (GSDs) who was out for his morning constitutional with his dogs on the lead, walked through a housing estate to the edge of a wood and, as was his normal practice, made the dogs sit before disconnecting the leads. As the dogs are trained for competition work, the owner makes them sit for some five or six seconds before releasing them to carry out their toilet requirements. During this five second spell the owner saw his dogs turn their heads to look behind. The owner also turned to see a Border Collie no more than ten paces away and running in fast as if to attack the GSDs. The Border Collie owner was some forty paces away and making no effort to recall his dog. The owner of the GSDs turned to tell his own dogs to stay, but in that fraction of a second the Border Collie was no more than five paces away and attacking fast. Under these conditions no dog is going to sit and wait to be attacked. Any dog in this situation is going to react in one of two ways: either he will run for his life or he will counter-attack.

The GSDs countered by chasing the Border Collie back into the housing estate and both owners had absolutely no control over the situation. Fortunately the GSDs were not fighters and came straight back after a fifty yard chase. I think this illustrates that the control an owner has over his dog is dependent on the nature of the situation and that a complete lack of consideration by one owner can affect a much more conscientious owner.

Control is also affected by the distance between dog and owner. Combined with the strength of the distraction, this creates a variability which is often taken as inconsistency in a dog's response. The greater the distance between dog and owner, the less control can be applied and the greater the distraction, the more difficult the situation becomes. Fortunately some dogs get worried at a distance and when they realise that their owners are far away they are only too keen to return.

4. Owner attentiveness

Many situations develop because an owner does not appreciate how quickly a pleasant walk can change into a situation beyond his control.

If we take the case of the GSDs and the Border Collie just described, there is no doubt that the owner of the Border Collie was responsible for this unpleasant situation. However, if the owner of the GSDs had looked behind him when he disconnected the leads he might have seen the other dog and the owner coming out of the wood and could have avoided the chase, but there is no doubt he would have had some other unpleasant situation to counter.

This particular case shows that dogs are much more conscious than owners of the presence of people or other animals. They can hear better, pick up a scent much better and at times can feel vibrations which are lost to our less sensitive senses. With these acute senses dogs will normally stop for a second to assess the situation before making a move. It is this momentary pause which owners fail to notice or appreciate. Action at that moment in time can often avoid the aggravation of an uncontrolled dog.

There are also the more obvious situations when a dog is allowed to wander out of a controlling distance and some distraction catches his attention. It may be a rabbit, a cat or children running past which activates a dog's interest: again control has been lost in a predictable situation.

Each owner should know the measure of control he can exert on his dog and under what conditions. Then he should do everything possible to ensure that he can maintain a balanced canine attitude.

There is also the case of the dog which eventually comes back but will run round the owner and cannot be caught. Unfortunately this situation is all too common and the key to the cause is in the complaint that the dog cannot be *caught*.

Young puppies can be caught, but as they grow older and more wily they can outrun their owners or dodge their grasping hands. To some dogs this becomes a game but with others it is the fear of retribution which creates the artful dodger. Chasing or grabbing will always create a problem for the future.

Remedial Action You Can Take

There are three important factors to keep in mind and to apply if recall problems are to be averted:

1. Make use of everyday situations to take advantage of natural and unsolicited recalls.
2. Carry out purposeful training to achieve an immediate response to your call.
3. Avoid calling your dog if you do not expect a cooperative response.

1. Natural situations

There are many occasions when normal canine activity lends itself to a recall. There are many times during a day when your dog makes unsolicited movements towards you: it may be for the pleasure of your company, you might be doing something which interests him or you might be getting his dinner ready. Do not take this return for granted, make a big thing of it, encourage him in with vocal and visual responses. Call him in to you, move backwards to induce a more urgent response as you use your hands and arms to indicate a welcome. Use titbits or toys if they are handy to reinforce your pleasure.

Although this approach on its own is unlikely to be fully effective with any dog who is beyond being a minor problem, it will help to establish a routine which will make purposeful training more effective.

2. Purposeful training

The attention-getting routine for the third target in Chapter Two is the real foundation for recall training and all three targets must be satisfactorily accomplished before progressing further.

Development can now be achieved via a flexi-lead, a thirty foot long line, a six foot short line and then complete freedom. The flexi-lead is not essential, although it can be very helpful, and progress can be attained via the thirty foot long line. With the flexi-lead attached to the collar, your dog should be given freedom to move away and show interest in some distraction within the full length of the line. Before the end of the line has been reached the stop button can be pressed as you call your dog, tug sharply and immediately move backwards, thereby applying the attention-getting routine. The flexi-lead cord will automatically retract and prevent the loose cord from catching in your dog's legs. When your dog is responding immediately without the need to press the stop button the flexi-lead can be replaced by the long line.

With the long thirty foot line attached to your dog's collar and allowed to drag along the ground, greater distances can be created between you and your dog than with the attention-getting routine or with the flexi-lead, but the line is available to be used as required.

The line should be allowed to drag along the ground. If your dog is rather excitable a piece of wood can be tied on to the free end to create tension. This in itself will often create a more responsible attitude from your dog. The larger the piece of wood the greater the sense of responsibility.

When your dog is showing interest in some distraction you should pick up the line, at some suitable distance from your dog, call his name, give a sharp tug on the line if necessary, and move backwards with encouraging overtures to induce the dog to follow.

The line should never be kept tight and your dog should never be pulled in at any stage. The line should be kept as low as is practical and should be utilised in the same manner as the lead during the attention-getting routine. As your dog comes in at a greater pace than you do moving backwards the extra line can be passed through your hands to ensure that you have control if your dog changes his mind. Great pleasure must be shown when your dog is back beside you.

This approach can be applied until it is certain that your dog will return from all forms and degrees of distraction. When this has been achieved, you should be able to call your dog back under various conditions without the need to pick up the line.

To have your dog come back is one thing, but to maintain his attention is quite another and it is now advisable to apply a form of control which keeps your dog happy and beside you.

The backward movement on the lead as applied during the early stages of the attention-getting routine can initially be applied with the reward of three or four titbits spaced every few seconds, along with both verbal and physical encouragement, to maintain your dog's attention. Your dog may stand or sit as he wishes. The objective at this stage is to maintain your dog's attention.

When this has been successfully achieved you should cut back to a single titbit but continue to try and maintain your dog's attention for a full five seconds. Any deviation of your dog's attention, due to a distraction or not, must immediately be countered with a quick backward movement for further attention getting. Always reward with praise – with or without titbits.

When your dog is responding consistently with satisfaction while on the lead you can carry out the same sequence of events using the long line to get your dog back. Control on a long line can then warrant changing to a six foot short line with a continuation of the same principles.

The importance of a successful and consolidated situation carried over from previous training will now become apparent and as with any other stage of training you must be prepared to go back to earlier stages if problems become evident.

Use of a short six foot line attached to the collar is the connecting link between the use of the long line and complete freedom. Apply the same principles as utilised with the long line but maintain short distances between the dog and you. Always avoid situations where a refusal can be expected. Build up the distance and minor distractions which are within your dog's capabilities and which correspond to his progress in training.

You may find it useful gradually to cut pieces off the length of cord as your confidence grows until only nine or ten inches are left. This gives your dog the feeling that the cord is still a controlling factor.

The ultimate and final objective is that of calling your dog to you while completely free and this is a continuation of the work to date. Again distances and the magnitude of the distraction should be built up slowly and carefully to avoid failure.

It must be remembered that success breeds confidence in yourself and control over your dog, but over-confidence has its own dangers. If this results in a failure you will need to go back to the six foot line, or even to the long line situation if necessary, to rebuild control and confidence. You are not required to remain stationary while your dog is coming in but can move backwards to help to induce an enthusiastic response.

As the fourth target of the attention-getting routine has already been accomplished, the use of titbits or a suitable toy will soon establish an attentive sit in front of you with sufficient time for praise before attaching the lead, if that is the purpose of the recall.

During normal exercise periods it is advisable to attach the long line to your dog before giving him freedom. Just let him pull the line behind and control can be attained by standing on the end or picking it up if necessary. The long line should be utilised until this full training programme has achieved the desired results. This may take up to three months.

3. Avoidance situations

During the purposeful training period care should be taken to avoid failure when out exercising your dog. This may appear to be a defeatist attitude but you should not call your dog in to you if a refusal is expected. Every failure to respond reinforces refusals and it is important to maintain a sequence of successes.

Assess the situation before calling your dog to you. If your dog is keyed in to a distraction, assess its possible effect and whether you can counter it. If necessary move to within a controlling distance and use everything you can to achieve success. This can mean using your voice (encouragement), hands and arms as you move away to induce your dog to return and, of course, titbits if they are going to help.

If you find that the situation has developed beyond your control and you cannot apply the recommended approach, consider it to be your own doing and avoid such situations in the future.

Preventive Measures You Can Take

Preventive measures are based on the approach already discussed under natural situations in this section. This approach, particularly with a young puppy, will create a strong foundation for a controlled but enjoyable future. The details under avoidance situations in this section can also help to ensure that uncontrolled situations are unlikely to develop.

An obedient puppy can change during the period of adolescence and can become very unreliable if the indications are not noted and acted upon. One failure leads to another and can soon become a habit. Act on the first indication of doubt in your dog's mind. When he appears to be thinking 'Do I go back or do I ignore him', that is the time to assess the degree of freedom your dog is being allowed and to limit it accordingly.

My own favoured outlook is that I would rather have my dog worried about my absence than worry about his. This attitude can be helped by playing hide and seek when out for a walk. Hide behind a tree, bush or other suitable obstacle when your dog is not watching. Hide in a manner in which you can observe your dog's reaction; if need be, call his name and watch him come back to find you. If he cannot find you, which is unlikely, come out into the open, call his name and when he sees you hide again. Make it fun and reward your dog every time he finds you. Rather than you worrying about your dog's wanderings it is more likely that he will keep an eye on you.

Problem 7.2 – NO CONTROL WHEN PLAYING WITH OTHER DOGS

When out walking, my dog will run away to play with other dogs. When he was a puppy we were advised to let him play with other dogs to ensure that he would be fully socialised and not aggressive with them.

An Understanding and Probable Causes

The advice given to this owner is good as far as it goes. It is certainly helpful to socialise a puppy with other dogs but unselective mixing with freedom to play has a number of very influential drawbacks:

1. Loss of control – too often this results in a form of independence where the puppy, or the dog when he matures, just does what he wants as and when he wants to do it. This brings us back to canine logic as described in Chapter One. When control has been lost anything can happen.

2. A puppy – particularly one of the larger breeds – during his period of growth can easily become over-excited, and freedom to play with other dogs can result in an excessive period of strenuous exercise. Two puppies can become over-excited and run around for lengthy periods before dropping exhausted, but a puppy playing with a more mature dog can be extended still further, as the older dog can carry on well beyond the puppy's reasonable period of exertion. Once the owners have lost control of the situation physical fatigue can cause its own problems and hyperactivity and excessive excitement can result from these sessions.

3. Loose dogs are rarely aggressive towards small puppies but these puppies grow up to become adults in a very short time and will continue to look for fun with other dogs. If the dog is loose and running free a dog on the lead with his owner can become an attraction. Dogs on the lead can feel restricted and may take up a defensive attitude – with dogs attack is the best means of defence when there is no escape route. Is it fair on other responsible dog owners to have a loose dog

bother their dogs while they are on the lead? It should also be recognised that some loose dogs can be very aggressive, but more about that in the chapter on aggression.

REMEDIAL AND PREVENTIVE ACTION YOU CAN TAKE

It will now be evident that indiscriminate freedom to play with other dogs can be the source of numerous problems, but socialising must still be given consideration.

Friends or acquaintances who have adult dogs who can be trusted and are controllable may provide the answer. Your youngster can be given freedom at times and in areas where he will not cause problems to other people. Your friends' dogs are the controlling factor and their ability to terminate a period of play before the youngster becomes exhausted should be utilised.

A full understanding of the training in Problem 7. 1 must also be appreciated and fully applied to achieve the desired control which should prevent undesirable situations from developing.

Problem 7.3 – CHASING CHILDREN AND JOGGERS

My dog can never resist the temptation to chase running children or joggers. Although he will not bite, the children are frightened and some of the joggers have created very unpleasant scenes.

AN UNDERSTANDING AND PROBABLE CAUSES

The excitement of the chase with the instinct of predators going in to catch their prey goes back before canine domestication when wild animals had to catch their next meal. This instinct has been purposely maintained in many breeds of dog through selective breeding for hunting, guarding and sport.

Greyhound racing is based on the strength of the instinct to chase and without this instinct the Border Collie would not make a good sheep herding dog, although in this breed the instinct to attack at the end of the chase has been controlled.

The gundog Pointer and Setter breeds have been selectively bred to indicate the vicinity of game but remain stationary in the presence of static or moving game. The instinct to chase has been completely suppressed through a discriminating choice in breeding.

It is, therefore, natural for many dogs, particularly when they are excited, to accept the challenge to chase running children. Joggers, by their very action, are also ideal targets for canine attention.

Many such chasers will not bite, but anybody being chased has reason to fear the consequences of being caught and this fear in itself may cause them to react in a manner which can induce some dogs to bite. Although a dog may chase today without biting, the same dog may undergo an experience at the end of the chase which will induce a bite on the next occasion.

Children, joggers or any other members of the public are entitled to run if they feel the desire or need to do so without the apprehension caused by the presence of a dog. This means that all dog owners must accept the responsibility of ensuring that their dogs are not going to chase.

REMEDIAL AND PREVENTIVE ACTION YOU CAN TAKE

Your own observation and control capabilities are the basis of the measures to be taken if future chasing is to be prevented.

A full understanding of the training detailed in Problem 7.1 is very important and the complete programme should be applied to achieve the control required; also it must be appreciated that a dog that has started to chase is very difficult to stop. It is, therefore, important that the application of control training and your own observation are essential ingredients in preventing the development or continuation of the chase instinct.

The problem described in Problem 6.5 can be the introduction to a more serious chasing problem at a later date and a study of this section may be of value.

Problem 7.4 – CHASING SHEEP

I used to enjoy walking in the country with my previous dog, as he had no inclination to chase sheep, rabbits or any other game. However, my present young dog will chase anything that moves. I do not mind him chasing rabbits and hares but he chases sheep when he gets the opportunity. Although it is just a game and he will not actually attack the sheep, I realise that farmers and shepherds will not be very pleased.

An Understanding and Probable Causes

It is quite understandable when farmers and shepherds are not very pleased at dogs chasing any of the animals in their charge, and I doubt if the sheep or any other farm animal (or bird) enjoys being chased by a dog. It should be recognised that today's chaser can easily become tomorrow's killer.

The predator instinct already described in Problem 7.3 is also relevant to this problem and the details should be studied. This owner does not mind his dog chasing rabbits but, in the dog's mind, the only difference between a rabbit and a sheep is the size. Dogs can be educated to understand that rabbits are fair game but sheep must be ignored – without that education anything that runs can be fair game for many dogs. It must be recognised that uncontrolled rabbit chasing can end in disaster: a road, a railway or a poacher's trap can terminate a chase with a dog being the victim.

The only things that dogs should be allowed or encouraged to chase are suitable toys. Balls (of the appropriate size), rubber rings, kongs, sticks and such things, which are thrown for them, should always provide the limitation and the outlet for this chasing instinct.

Remedial and Preventive Action You Can Take

As with the other problems described in this chapter, your observation and control capabilities are vital if prevention is to be your objective.

I could recommend repeating the measures described in Problem 7.3 which, of course, relates to other relevant problems. Although I feel that this basic training is of great value for this particular type of problem, the easiest and most sensible solution is to take avoiding action. That is, to maintain control by means of a lead, a flexi-lead or long line when you are in the vicinity of sheep or other farm animals. This is probably the easiest and simplest way of preventing situations from getting out of control. Farmers and shepherds will also appreciate the consideration.

Problem 7.5 – CHASING MOTOR VEHICLES AND BICYCLES

My dog chases motor cars and motor bikes at every opportunity. He will even chase a pedal cyclist if he gets the chance.

AN UNDERSTANDING AND PROBABLE CAUSES

This is probably a defensive action: if a vehicle or bicycle passes his patch, the dog feels that it must be chased. Some people may consider this to be a predatory reaction and they may be correct. The canine logic behind the dog's actions is not too important but prevention of the problem is.

Success in chasing a motor vehicle off his patch can create the confidence in the dog which induces him to chase the next one away. This becomes a habit and any form of motorised transport which passes then becomes fair game.

Again, as with other chasing problems, the dog is very difficult to stop when he is actually chasing the vehicle.

REMEDIAL AND PREVENTIVE ACTION YOU CAN TAKE

Some young dogs seem to have this chasing instinct when they first meet traffic while they are out for a walk on the lead. In cases of this nature the corrective measures detailed in Problem 6.1 relating to pulling on the lead should be applied.

I make no attempt to advise on how to cure dogs who chase vehicles on the road except to say that no dog should be out and near a road without being on the lead. A loose dog near a road is a danger to himself, but he is a greater danger to road users and can cause an accident. Keep your dog under full control when near a road and he cannot chase any type of vehicle.

CHAPTER EIGHT

Aggression Problems

Canine aggression is probably the most worrying of all problems and it is the condition which many owners do not like to talk about until there is an immediate risk of losing their dogs because of this type of behaviour. All too often the knowledge of canine aggression towards the owner or family member in the home is kept within the family and only when the situation becomes impossible does the owner look for expert assistance.

Many dogs will guard their food, their favourite chair or even the matrimonial bed from a husband who spends periods working away from home. Canine aggression is often limited to visitors, people in the street or other dogs. Postmen, milk boys or the paper delivery girl are often targets for aggressive canine reactions.

Aggression is based on dominance as the dog's permanent objective, although fear will cause temporary and short-term attempts at domination and, therefore, an aggressive attitude in situations where he sees no alternative.

There is seldom a situation within a domestic environment when a dog should be permitted to show his aggression to the degree of actually attacking, and there is often a very fine dividing line between a show of aggression and the actual attack. It might be a slight change in circumstances which results in a warning developing into an attack.

Aggression or the indications of an offensive attitude can be placed into three categories:

1. Protective – over family and property. Although many breeds will act in this manner the guarding breeds are specialists in this function.
2. Possessive – Many dogs can become very possessive over items which they believe to be their own property, food, toys, favourite chair, etc.
3. Fear-based – This is often a condition of nervousness inherited through breeding, but owners can and do contribute to the situation by creating too sheltered an existence. However, like ourselves, dogs are, on occasion, taken by surprise and the temporary fear of a situation can cause flight or aggression as a reaction.

Each of these categories must be taken seriously. Aggressive canine actions can affect people, dogs or other animals. As we all know, loss of life, injury and mental trauma can result from a canine aggressive reaction to a situation.

Barking when associated with an aggressive canine attitude should be considered as an aggression problem and treated within the appropriate category. Barking is most commonly associated with the protective designation, although fear can also be the cause of such a vocal canine response. Possessiveness does not usually create a barking reaction from a dog but growling is a common reaction. Barking as a result of excitement is quite another matter and has been dealt with quite separately in Problem 5.9.

Although an owner may be concerned about an individual problem within one of the situations described, it would be advisable to read and digest the full contents of this chapter.

An owner's control over his dog is a vital factor when considering aggression problems and the lack of sufficient control is probably the most common cause of unwarranted and unpleasant canine reactions. It is stressed very strongly that the training routines in Chapter Two are applied to ensure that the dog is highly responsive to basic control requirements.

Aggressive behaviour problems with male dogs, particularly when involving aggression against other dogs, can be due to an imbalance of sex hormones and castration may well be the answer.

This can be a very emotive subject and I always feel that veterinary advice should be sought when trying to isolate the cause of this problem. Consequently, I believe that each case *must* be treated individually by the people who know best and are likely to give the soundest advice.

Problem 8.1 – PROTECTIVE AGGRESSION

I have a young dog who was very friendly with people when he was a puppy. He is now just over a year old and will bark viciously at anybody who comes to the house. One day the postman put his fingers through the letter box as he delivered the mail and the dog bit him. I have been warned that a repetition of this type of action will result in a court appearance.

An Understanding and Probable Causes

One of the greatest assets in owning a dog is his ability to warn the owner of the presence of another person. In the home, be it the house or the garden, some dogs give warning by becoming excited or barking a welcome to a visitor while others will take up a protective stance and bark in a much more meaningful manner. The latter is the type of dog that may eventually become truly aggressive and, therefore, a problem if control and canine responsibility are not achieved.

Unfortunately, many owners encourage their dogs at an early age to become 'warning' dogs in and about the home and then find that they cannot control the situation. The 'warning' dog can quickly and easily turn into a 'protection' dog, one which will bite first and let the owner answer for his actions later.

It is often felt that the guarding breeds are the most likely dogs to go wrong and protect in a positive and aggressive manner. However, it is the smaller breeds and the terrier families which seem to be the least controlled and most aggressively active of all breeds. No breed is safe from criticism although it may be the type of owner who has caused some of the reputed softer breeds to become aggressive.

The type of owner does have a lot to do with a dog's aggressive tendencies, although breeding can be an important factor. The responsible owners generally control the situations but the macho image of some owners with guarding breeds can create situations which develop beyond their experience of control. The dog will bark or guard and is encouraged by the owner because he wants to show that his dog will protect him. However, most of these owners do not know how to terminate this show of aggression and the dog finally takes full control.

A number of female dog owners feel that they require the protection of their dogs and act in a similar manner to the macho owners. Although their purpose is not to show off but purely one of protection the results are the same. The dog decides to take over and the owner is helpless to prevent the unpleasant and unfortunate result.

Some small dog owners do not see their pets as being a danger to other people: some think it quite amusing to see their little dogs indicate a show of aggression, but many a postman has had good reason to complain of the resulting canine action.

Lap dogs or toy breeds which are carried round by their owners can become extremely protective of them. They become responsible for their owners and seldom show any responsibility to them.

Unfortunately owners' reactions to aggressive canine attitudes are generally completely wrong or totally inadequate. All too often owners are heard to apply a sympathetic voice and attitude to their dogs while they hold them on a tight lead or by the collar. This is only going to encourage the aggressive attitude. Other owners will give a gentle verbal scolding and again hold a tight lead. The inadequacy of this approach is evident by the lack of an effective result.

A dog in an aggressive state of mind will only understand and respond responsibly to a matching aggressive attitude from the owner. This does not mean that the owner should resort to uncontrolled violence or to hitting the dog, but it does require a very dominating attitude when the purpose is to overcome an attempt at canine aggression.

Postmen, milkmen and others who visit the house to make some sort of delivery without actually meeting dog and owner, unconsciously, and by the nature of this function, help to encourage and draw on the guarding instincts with these dogs. As the delivery person comes towards the house the dog barks as a warning and is probably telling the 'intruder' not to come any closer. If the 'intruder' is a milk delivery man he leaves the milk on the door step and walks away. The dog consequently thinks that his aggressive stance has chased the 'intruder' off his premises and this will encourage a more confident and spirited attitude next time.

If the 'intruder' is a postman and the dog has access to the front door, the same reaction occurs, but the dog may then vent his aggression on the postman's fingers as he delivers the mail through the letter box. Fingers may become the object of the aggressive attack or, with the postman's scent on the mail from his normal handling of the letters which drop at the dog's feet, the mail may well become the subject of the dog's attention. Many a letter has been destroyed this way.

Delivery people, while acting normally, have no control of the situation. Unfortunately, a number of these 'intruders' will act aggressively towards the dog when they know that they have the safety of a brick wall or fence between themselves and the dog. A milkman may tease a dog from such a position and the postman may suffer as a result when he delivers a parcel by hand. An innocent person can be on the receiving end due to some other person's stupidity.

At the end of the day it is the owner's responsibility to control the effect of normal, or abnormal, activity of delivery personnel. It should also be recognised that any warning bark or growl can be interpreted as the first stage in the development of more active canine aggression. Remember that the failure to control canine aggressive reactions can result in a court appearance if owners attempt to defend their dogs' activities.

REMEDIAL ACTION YOU CAN TAKE

The remedial action for aggressiveness towards people may well depend on the actual conditions and three basic situations will be discussed:

1. Reaction to a delivery person.
2. Reaction to a visitor who comes into the house.
3. Reaction to meeting people when out for a walk.

It must be recognised that you can only achieve satisfactory results if you are accepted by your dog as the pack leader. He must respect your authority; he must trust you as a person who will be consistent and fair in your dealings with him. There is no 'softly, softly' approach under these conditions and when the first signs of an aggressive situation develop, you must create the circumstances in which your dog will appreciate that the likely outcome is going to be unpleasant.

I have already stated that a dog only understands aggression against him as a means of countering his own aggressive tendencies and it is essential that this reasoning is understood and accepted. Control training is essential and the application of the training routines in Chapter Two is an important ingredient for ensuring your ability to control aggressive situations.

1. Reaction to a delivery person
Initially it is important to observe the actions and reactions of the various delivery people and refuse collectors when they come to the house. A milkman or even a postman may aggravate a barking dog from the safety of a door or fence and create an antagonistic pet. If this is the case, a word in the right place may help to prevent this unwarranted human behaviour being repeated. This knowledge and advertising the fact may well be vital if your dog does commit an aggressive offence as a result of human inconsideration. However, we wish to avoid such situations and preventive measures must be taken. It would be sensible to restrict your dog's movements so that he cannot see the delivery person and also to have more than one wall or door between him and the 'intruder's' line of approach. If the postman is the subject of your dog's attention, he can be kept from the door area until the mail delivery has been made. The further your dog is from the 'intruder' the less aggressive his attitude is likely to be.

Many owners want their dogs to bark so that unwanted intruders will stay away but dogs cannot be expected to know the difference between legitimate 'intruders' and others, although consistent sequences of events will tell many dogs who to expect at particular times of the day. Expert control and a balanced canine upbringing are required before considering the application of any guarding qualities in your dog. If you wish to have a 'guard dog' at home, it is recommended that you read *All About Guard Dogs and Their Training* (John Cree), published by Pelham Books.

Problem 5.9 on barking dogs has discussed the methods of dealing with a dog who barks when delivery or other visitors come to the door. Our problem with the aggressive dog is an extension of this problem but it must be recognised as being more serious. The use of the six foot line attached to your dog's collar so that he can trail it behind him is the most suitable approach. A strong lead of some four to six feet in length may be used instead of a line to ensure that a proper hold can be maintained.

With the first signs of agitated canine activity and if possible, before real aggression appears, pick up the end of the line or lead, move backwards quickly and apply a jerk at the end of the line as you call your dog's name and *demand* his attention. The strength of all these actions is dependent on your dog's expected responses. Your physical and vocal effort with the speed of your backward movement must have the strength and purpose which will achieve the desired result. This is attention getting at its extreme. The moment you achieve success give your dog abundant praise and rewards if appropriate.

Move forward again with line in hand and try to maintain your dog's attention on yourself. If the visitor is still in the vicinity and your dog returns to an aggressive attitude, repeat the strong attention-getting process as before. It is important that your dog should not be allowed to strain on the end of the line, or be held by the collar, nor should he be pulled back on the end of the lead: such a form of restraint will only make the situation worse.

As mentioned in Problem 5.9 other methods may be effectively utilised on their own or in conjunction with the attention-getting routine to shake your dog out of his aggressive dominance. The banging of two baking tins right behind him can make him alert to your requirements and induce a more responsive attitude. A squirt of clean water from a squeezy bottle or the use of a mugger/rape alarm may also prove to be effective.

It is very unlikely that any pleasant approach is going to achieve the desired results; it is the proper and consistent use of more demanding methods which is going to control the situation. However, the strong vocal and physical approach must always be applied sensibly and should be followed immediately by praise for a cooperative response when it succeeds.

If it is possible to have your dog meet delivery people with safety where they can get to know each other it can help, but I doubt if many individuals will be happy to cooperate in this.

2. Reaction to a visitor who comes into the house
The basic principles for the reaction to a delivery person apply in this type of case, the difference being that the person will be coming into the house or garden and will remain there for a period of time.

Everything that has been written in the section about reactions to delivery people must, therefore, be applied if your dog is to be allowed into the presence of the visitor. It must be said that to continually avoid allowing your dog to meet a visitor can make him worse when he does meet someone in the house or even when he meets people out in the street.

After applying the attention-getting routine with the strength required by using the six foot line or a suitable lead and any of the other aids suggested, it may be possible to let your visitor into the house while controlling your dog on a loose lead. This will depend on the control you have achieved and the understanding nature of your visitor. Some visitors will not be happy about being introduced to a dog that they do not trust and they should not be subjected to such a situation, unless they are visitors you would rather do without.

On the other hand, it may be advisable to have your dog in another room until the visitor is settled and then to introduce your dog while on the short line or lead. At this stage the visitor should ignore your dog completely and not even look at him. Any sign of aggression should immediately be countered by the forceful attention-getting routine. You can also give the visitor a bag of titbits to hold and when you feel that the conditions are right, let the end of the line go and give your dog freedom to inspect your visitor. The visitor should still ignore your dog. If he shows interest in the bag of titbits, your visitor should take one out of the bag and let him come close to investigate the titbit in the clenched fist. He can then open his hand with the palm upwards and let the dog help himself. A few more titbits presented in this manner will help to give both dog and visitor confidence that everything is all right.

Until you are happy about your dog's expected reaction when your visitor leaves it would be wise to put your dog in another room while the visitor makes his departure.

Forcefulness to counter aggression and kindness to indicate your pleasure form the basis of your corrective procedure.

3. Reaction to meeting people when out for a walk
This situation can develop with some dogs while they are on the lead but not when free, or the situation can be reversed; some dogs can also be aggressive under both conditions.

A dog who shows aggression towards people when off the lead should not be given freedom to do so at any time. The dog should be kept on the lead or a long dragging line and within a controlling distance.

The procedure for correcting this problem is based on the attention-getting approach described under the conditions relating to people visiting the home, with the forcefulness already described being an essential element. The general approach described in Problem 6.5 covering snapping at people passing also applies and this problem should be fully studied.

It is often said that dogs who behave aggressively while in the company of their owners are being responsible *for* their owners and not *to* them. It is important that dogs trust the judgement of their owners and become responsible *to* them instead of needlessly protecting them.

Preventive Measures You Can Take

Creating opportunities for a puppy to mix with people can be the best preventive measure to take, but mixing does not mean complete freedom. Canine aggression is often created by other people's lack of consideration, or by their own fear of dogs. A puppy running up to and playfully jumping up at a person can be hit, kicked or otherwise upset by a human reaction and this can be the start of a retaliative aggressive reaction. The fault does not lie with the passer-by but with the owner who allowed his dog such uncontrolled freedom.

The first sign of aggressive barking or growling must be countered immediately in a short, positive and unpleasant manner with instant praise for a satisfactory reaction. A full understanding of the remedies will help you to react positively and appreciatively.

Problem 8.2 – POSSESSIVE AGGRESSION

My dog has now become very possessive with his toys and food; he will growl and even bite if I go too close to him in certain situations. Because he has already bitten me once when I went to pick up a food overspill beside his dinner dish while he was eating, I am now frightened to go near him when he takes up his possessive stance and growls at me.

An Understanding and Probable Causes

This type of problem causes one of the most embarrassing situations that any dog owner has to contend with. Nobody likes to admit that his dog bites the hand that feeds him.

A multitude of different situations can bring possessiveness into the open. It may be food, the dog's toys, his favourite armchair, the matrimonial bed or even the fact that the dog is touched in some tender spot.

The reaction is generally a warning growl but some dogs dispense with this formality and go straight in with a single bite. It is not only the owner who is at risk: other members of the family or even the general public who happen to be in the wrong place at the wrong time are likely to become victims. However, this type of dog seldom maintains an attack and generally considers one bite to be sufficiently effective to maintain his dominance and possession of the item he wishes to control.

Some dogs seem to be full of remorse immediately after an unwarranted attack, but this apparent remorse should not be a reason for instant forgiveness because the incident is likely to recur if positive action is not taken.

Too often canine aggression is considered to be symbolic of guarding breeds but some of the smaller and common pet breeds are more prone to possessive aggressiveness. I am reluctant to name breeds with problems but two favourite breeds with the sweetest of natures come to mind: the Cocker Spaniel and the Golden Retriever are two of the most suited breeds for a full family life and yet certain strains in breeding combined with weak or inexperienced ownership can allow natural possessiveness to become aggressively active. I would not wish to put anybody off these breeds which are so suited to family life, but one must illustrate that even within the most lovable breeds problems can occur.

Quite often the symptoms are there in puppyhood. Some owners think it funny to have a little puppy growl and will even tease it in a manner which brings out this aggressiveness. The damage has been done at this early stage in a dog's life. Maturity brings out dominance and the inevitable attack on some unfortunate person. It may not be the member of the family who created the situation but some innocent and unsuspecting member of the public.

Fear is the owner's biggest handicap and the dog's confidence builder. So long as the person who is the receiver of this possessive aggressiveness is frightened to act positively and with courage the dog will act in a manner which he considers to be in his best interest and will gain strength from his success. Such success can lead to the dog's destruction.

REMEDIAL ACTION YOU CAN TAKE

As already stated in Problem 8.1 canine aggression must be countered by human aggression to create the change in dominance. It is not carried out with brutality, malice or in a fit of temper, although I have advised a few owners to *pretend* that they have lost their tempers for a three second vocal burst to create the measure of human posturing which will achieve success.

Your response is dependent on the situation which has developed, but most people are caught off guard and do not have time to think about a response suited to the occasion. A history of previous events can help you prepare for the next one so that you may plan and act instantly in the most suitable manner.

Submission is the name of the game and at any sign of canine aggression – be it just a curl of the lip or a quiet growl – the dog must be made to submit to your dominance. A very short vocal blast may be quite sufficient to achieve normality or it may be necessary to take the dog by the scruff of the neck and shake him or, if possible, to get him down on the ground to achieve a submissive response. This takes courage and the more positive your approach, the more successful the result.

As with any other unpleasant action on your part, it must be short and sharp, then immediately followed by kindness and praise as soon as your dog responds.

The attention-getting training routine in Chapter Two to the second target is most important. If you have a real fear of being bitten because you doubt you will be able to react in a suitable and effective manner to your dog's aggression the attachment of the short line can make correction much easier.

The short line can be attached to your dog's collar and left to drag round while you are at home. The offending situations may be at feeding time, while he has a bone or when he has settled on your favourite chair. Whatever the situation, when an aggressive reaction is expected, pick up the end of the line and give a sharp, purposeful tug as you call your dog's name and move backwards. Keep his attention on yourself with vocal and visual encouragement as you move backwards as far as you wish. You can go out of the room if necessary. Stop and give your dog praise for giving you his attention: a titbit or some reward would not be out of place. Just let him know that you are pleased with his attentive reaction.

If the cause of the situation is possessiveness over a toy or his food, let your dog go back to the cause and assess his reaction to your presence. Your attention-getting procedure may have to be repeated on a number of occasions, but success is only achieved when you can pick up his dish or toy without an aggressive response. Always praise your dog for not reacting aggressively and give him back the dish or toy.

The procedure for dogs who commandeer the bed or chair is similiar, but do not encourage him back on to them. Just wait for the next time he goes on of his own accord; eventually the sharp edge of your tongue will be sufficient to achieve the desired result.

The aids applied in Problem 5.9 and 8.1 can also be effectively utilised. The banging of two baking tins right beside your dog as you give a strong vocal reprimand can be effective. A squirt of clean water or the use of a mugger/rape alarm may also prove to be effective. However, praise should always follow a successful result.

PREVENTIVE MEASURES YOU CAN TAKE

Prevention is based on watching for the very first sign of possessive aggressiveness. A curl of the lips or a low growl must be caught right away with a sharp vocal reprimand or/and a grip of your dog's collar or loose skin at his neck. A short sharp shake at his neck should be sufficient. Never think his aggressive posture is funny and never think that he will grow out of it. He is more likely to continue and become more dominant in the situations where he feels he is the leader of the family pack.

Problem 8.3 – FEAR-BASED AGGRESSION

My dog is very timid and, when on the lead, he will try to bite anybody who wishes to be friendly and touch him. He has already bitten a friend who bent down to pat him.

AN UNDERSTANDING AND PROBABLE CAUSES

The breeding from shy and unsound parentage is all too often the cause of frightened dogs, although this is not always the case.

The failure to have a puppy in the nest accustomed to being handled and by a variety of people, especially supervised children, can be a sizeable handicap in trying to socialise a growing youngster.

Even after the nest stage puppies are often restricted to kennels with little or no socializing during the critical period in their young lives. A puppy taken into a domestic environment between seven to ten weeks of age has the best opportunity of coping with life as it happens. Each week after this tenth week increases the possibility of environmental problems. The actual age of a puppy leaving the breeder and the effect of this environmental change is going to be dependent on breeding and the earlier environmental circumstances.

One puppy that I bought could not be brought home until he was fifteen weeks old but, by agreement, the breeder carried out a socialising programme to minimise the effect of the eventual change and to give the puppy a foundation for the future. The breeding was sound and the socialising was carried out satisfactorily – the result was an excellent companion for the whole of his life.

Unfortunately sympathy and sheltering from the fearful interactions of socialisation can only create a more stressful situation for the dog when simple everyday conditions are presented to him.

The snarling, growling or barking which can result in biting are generally warnings that the dog feels the need to protect himself or attempts at temporary dominance as a means of self-preservation. If a dog feels cornered or if he is on the lead and cannot manoeuvre out of a situation which concerns him, he may well show this dominance because of fear.

Any owner who tries to sympathise with his dog is in fact telling the dog that he is correct for acting in such a manner and is encouraging a repeat performance under similar circumstances.

Punishment, cruelty or unwarranted and excessive unpleasantness towards a puppy or older dog will create a measure of fear and if the dog is shy or submissive apprehension of a recurrence might prompt an aggressive reaction.

Breeding, socialising and owner reactions are the factors which create the resultant canine character – be it good or bad.

REMEDIAL ACTIONS YOU CAN TAKE

Overcoming fear is the prime objective and this is achieved by giving your dog confidence to face day-to-day situations. Your size, relative to your dog, your vocal approach and your physical or visual attitude can affect your dog's reactions. The same factors applied to other people who come into contact with your dog will have the same effect.

To stand beside a frightened dog can be very disconcerting but to sit on the ground beside him and to appear much smaller can, within a short time, remove his apprehension. A demanding tone of voice can frighten lesser humans, never mind a fearful dog, but a soft gentle voice can have a soothing effect. An aggressive human stance or sharp body movements can give the appearance of unwarranted human dominance and again create a fearful canine creature. However, a gentle human posture with compatible body movements can have a very relaxing effect on a worried dog.

Forward movement towards a frightened dog is likely to make him more frightened, but moving slowly away in an enticing manner can help to achieve a calmer atmosphere and a more relaxed dog. A happy, carefree, although not exciting, atmosphere can generally help to create a relaxed canine outlook and should reduce the tension within the dog.

The use of titbits or play toys can often make a dog forget his fear of the situation and a combination of human stature, voice control with exciting rewards and backward human movement can help many dogs to overcome their fear of the various environmental situations which trouble them. Giving attention to a frightened dog can on occasion create a greater build-up of stress and increase the probability of an aggressive reaction, perhaps not at that moment, but at some future date when something in his mind snaps and he feels that he must act to protect himself against an imaginary interference to his own security. Too often people force themselves on to dogs and create the situation which has just been explained.

Many dogs will accept visitors or people they are uncertain of when these visitors ignore them. When eye-to-eye contact is avoided and physical expression – such as extended arms to induce the dog forward – are also avoided, an uncertain or frightened dog can become curious and eventually want attention. When this happens a visitor can hold a bag of titbits in his hand or even the favourite play toy. When the dog shows interest, eye-to-eye contact should still be avoided and no appreciable physical movement should be made towards the dog. However, titbits or the toy can be made available by the visitor. This can initially be done by dropping them on the floor and eventually by having the dog take them from the visitor's hand.

By applying this general approach your dog will gain a measure of confidence, and visitors or acquaintances you meet in the street can start to take a little interest in your dog's inviting actions or reactions.

There are occasions when you may be able to leave your dog, on the lead, with a visitor. The visitor should be handed the lead at arm's length to create distance between you and the visitor. When you have moved away and out of the immediate area – say into another room or the garden – the visitor should sit at ground level and ignore the dog until he reacts as previously described. After a very short and stressful period many dogs respond very well to this procedure. Your visitor should only act when your dog is responding, even if that response is only to calm down. It is important to recognise that some dogs get into such a state in the presence of any visitor that expert help may be required to assess the measure of success which can be expected. Success is often related to people's ability to react properly and to assess the rate of progress.

If at any time your dog does dart forward to indicate aggression, you must act forcibly to dominate and terminate this reaction. The attention-getting training routine to the second target of Chapter Two can be very helpful in achieving results. When your dog is on or off the lead use a strong and uncompromising vocal reaction to terminate his aggression; if on the lead, also use the necessary jerk. Your reaction must be short and sharp, and the second you get your dog's attention move backwards with abundant praise and a reward if available. You do not want your dog to be frightened of you, but you must have a respectful reaction. Off the lead is not as easy but the same principle applies.

PREVENTIVE MEASURES YOU CAN TAKE

Prevention starts by choosing a young puppy from parents of sound temperament and also by socialising at an early age. It is appreciated that puppies cannot be taken out into the street until fully inoculated but plenty of visitors, especially children, or visits to friends by car can help to lay a sound foundation.

Any signs of your puppy withdrawing from situations may indicate hereditary weakness or it may be that you are expecting too much from a young inexperienced dog.

Do not pressurise your youngster into stressful situations but avoid an over-protective attitude. Do not sympathise if the situation gets too much for him, laugh it off and create pleasant distractions to ensure that the memory of these pleasant distractions is more prominent than the cause of the distressing situation.

Problem 8.4 – AGGRESSION TOWARDS OTHER DOGS

While out on the lead my dog becomes very aggressive towards any dog we meet, particularly if the other dog is free to come too close to my own. When I have touched him to get his attention he has turned to try to bite me.

An Understanding and Probable Causes

Aggression, when it happens, usually takes place between two male dogs or two bitches. It is seldom that a male will continue an aggressive attitude against a bitch when he realises her sex. However, a bitch may well continue an aggressive attitude against a male dog, who usually backs down, if she feels his intent has amorous inclinations.

Two dogs in the one house can frequently have very meaningful aggressive tantrums: again, with two males together – even litter brothers – one can try to become the dominant member of the canine family and as a consequence some serious fights ensue with resulting injuries. The same can be said for two bitches within a single household, although fights between bitches can be more vicious and damaging. Within the home, contesting for pack leadership or jealousy are the principal causes. If there is one dominant and one submissive animal in the family, meaningful aggression is very rare, although play fighting may be an enjoyable part of their lives. If there is a similar degree of dominance between two males or two bitches, skin and hair can fly from time to time. This problem is unlikely to be evident between an adult and a puppy but all puppies grow up to become adults and may well wish to change the balance of domination.

Whether in the home or in the street canine aggression is very upsetting to owners and it can be difficult or, on many occasions, may even be impossible to reconcile dogs who cannot sort out their pecking order without intermittent fights.

Going back to dogs that are aggressive while out for a walk, it is often the case of a dog feeling restricted on the lead which causes the problem. No dog feels free to show his true character while on the lead. If he is let off the lead he may show a dominating stature without aggression and, thereby, achieve his objective. On the other hand, his aggression may be through fear, and while on the lead he will only show aggression towards dogs who are running free. The same dog may well ignore a passing dog who is on the lead.

Aggression is often a form of guarding: the dog is protecting his own provider and no other dog is going to share his pack leader. If given the opportunity this type of dog will chase another dog off his patch, which can be a twenty or thirty yard radius round his owner. Once the stray dog has been chased away the dog will come back to his owner very pleased with himself, as if to say 'I got rid of him for you'. A dog may act in this manner on his own daily walking territory but may be quite subdued when walking in an area which is strange to him.

Owners do get bitten by their own dogs when they try to interfere with their dogs' aggressive postures. A dog who has set himself up for a fight will not tolerate any interference from behind and will immobilise the weak opposition (the owner) so that he can concentrate on the adversary.

REMEDIAL ACTION YOU CAN TAKE

This is one situation where avoiding action when possible is an important part of the overall solution. Avoiding confrontation between two dogs is much better than allowing aggressive attitudes to prevail. It is fully understood that this approach is far from being the complete solution to the problem, but it is a good starting point.

Many theorists and experts will give the opposite advice and recommend that dogs should sort out their own problems and when dominance has been established between two adversaries peace will reign. This theory goes back to the pack situation in the wild when the less dominant animal (in losing a confrontation) can and does submit or takes flight. He or she may never return to the pack, may become a loner or may start another pack as the dominant leader. The animal might return to the pack and remain a subordinate member until he feels strong enough to make a challenge on an ageing leader. This less dominant animal has many options: the domestic pet in the home or kennel does not have these options. Although some power struggles can be sorted out by allowing dogs to get on with it, I feel that this is a very dangerous situation to encourage. Many a dog has been ruined for life because of the advice of theorists.

With two dogs in the home who fight, some theorists also say that the underdog should not receive any sympathy or petting but the dominant dog should. This prevents further jealousy from the dominant dog and reduces the possibility of further confrontations. The theory is sound and can help to create a peaceful atmosphere. However, I, for one, do not have the type of nature to ignore the underdog and give my affection to the bossy, dominant and aggressive canine companion. I believe that most dog owners feel as I do and cannot carry out this theory in practice.

I have no simple answer for dogs that fight in the home. It may well be that they should never be left together without dominant supervision. Any owner in this situation *must* be aware of situations which are likely to develop into a confrontation and terminate the situation immediately through his own dominance. The soundest answer may well be to part with one of the dogs so that each of them can receive the love and affection they both deserve in their respective homes.

What should an owner do when a fight between two dogs does occur in the home, garden or kennel? To enter the fray as the dominant contender and with an aggressive attitude which will make both dogs submit is one answer if the owner has the courage and ability to tackle such a situation successfully without becoming the victim of canine aggression.

It must be recognised that dogs can become very insensitive to pain and the peripheral factors during a fight. Any human at the site of an aggressive confrontation is such a factor unless he can make a significant impression on the principal adversary.

However, there are aids which can help to make an impression on fighting dogs. The banging of two baking tins over the dogs, the use of a mugger/rape alarm or a jet of water can be very effective, especially if this is accompanied by strong verbal abuse to reinforce your displeasure.

Controlling an aggressive dog on the lead and achieving a submissive canine outlook cannot be attained while the dog is pulling on the lead. If your dog is pulling and growling or barking at another dog you must take action to attract your dog's undivided attention to yourself and away from the other dog. You must become the dominating factor in the situation. The training detailed in the attention-getting routine to the second target in Chapter Two becomes an essential requirement.

Any indications of an aggressive posture from your dog should immediately be countered as forcibly as necessary by applying the backward movement and having your dog follow you attentively with his back to the adversary. You must dominate the scene but give praise for a satisfactory reaction. This praise may result in a return to aggressive posturing towards the original cause. If this happens, repeat the backward movement until your full objective has been achieved.

PREVENTIVE MEASURES YOU CAN TAKE

A sound choice of breeding or of breed can minimise the possibility of having a puppy or dog which is going to become aggressive. Consideration of other canine companions in the home must also be a factor. Remember that there is seldom trouble between a dog and a bitch in the same home.

Avoiding action should always be considered to minimise the possibility of an aggressive confrontation and suitable training should be carried out to ensure that control can be applied when the situation demands it.

When passing another dog owner in the street always make sure that your body is between your dog and that of the other dog. If both parties have their dogs walking at their left side as per loose lead training routines then the two owners are between the dogs and thereby create a more controllable situation.

CHAPTER NINE

Miscellaneous Problems

The problems discussed in the previous chapters have been grouped to help establish related topics and, therefore, to give the reader an opportunity of gaining a wider perspective of his own particular problem.

It may be felt that some of the problems discussed in this chapter can be related to at least one of the general topics already mentioned, but the situations suggest that they be given treatment within a chapter which caters for a wider field of events.

Problem 9.1 – DOGS AND CHILDREN

My ten-year-old son and our puppy do not seem to get on together. When the puppy was very young the two of them were great friends but now that the puppy is almost a year old, he growls at my son when he comes into the room. I feel, at times, that the puppy is going to attack and bite my son and I am very worried at this change in the relationship.

AN UNDERSTANDING AND PROBABLE CAUSES

A dog can be the greatest asset to a family of children and most dogs enjoy this lifestyle to the full. Unfortunately, some puppies do not have the temperament to stand up to the hurly-burly existence of noisy, overactive children and some children are not sufficiently understanding to share the same home as a puppy.

This subject has a much wider inference than the problem stated and children can be their own worst enemies. Children have friends and pals: they have fun and a close relationship one minute and because of some thoughtless or selfish act, they become enemies the next. They may fight or just call each other names but the bitterness may be forgotten after a night's sleep. They can be the best of pals again or bitterness and spite may linger for a long, long time. Children can hold a grudge and act in a sneaky, unpleasant manner when nobody is paying attention to them.

Unfortunately, many young dogs are not so understanding if they are treated badly by children. A child may pull a dog's tail, give him a kick or hit him with a stick or tease him when nobody is looking and then the parents wonder why the dog dislikes their son or daughter. It is not that the dog is unforgiving: because he cannot understand changing moods or inconsistent actions, he is uncertain of the response to expect from such a child.

I recall one family where a German Shepherd puppy was bought for a twelve-year-old daughter. The agreement and understanding between the parents and child was that she would share the responsibility of bringing up and caring for the puppy. She would take her turn at feeding and exercising him.

When the puppy was about eight months old (and the novelty of having a puppy had worn off) he would cower and growl with fear when the daughter came into the room. The girl became frightened of the puppy and eventually it had to go.

In the meantime, investigation into the cause of the problem revealed the true situation. If the puppy needed to be taken out in the evening for his toilet requirements and it was the daughter's turn to attend to it, she objected if a television programme caught her interest. However, the rules of the house meant that she had to take her turn. The daughter's spite was vented on the puppy and he was heard to give a cry when taken out of the house. It was assumed that the puppy was hit or kicked for the trouble he was causing. As he progressed to a stage of adolescence the puppy showed his distrust and dislike for this horrible child. This dog went into a new home but never trusted children and was eventually put to sleep because this distrust resulted in him biting an innocent child.

General excitability can cause an overreaction from a puppy or on occasion from an older dog. Children can become excited, jump around, wave their hands and arms with fast and jerky movements. An excited dog may well bite in fun or he may feel that his own special pal is being attacked by a visiting chum and give a meaningful bite as a measure of protection. There are many reasons for young dogs, in particular, being blamed for a natural reaction when they are left in a situation which should have been foreseen by a responsible adult.

Children are often allowed to take or are sent out with the family dog for exercise or a walk. When out for a walk with my own dogs, I have witnessed some of these children with an uncontrollable or aggressive dog on the lead. Most children do not have the strength or ability to control the dog who is determined to attack or play with another dog. I have seen children in tears because of frustration or with a sore hand because the dog was pulling too hard on his lead. A bit more thought and consideration from a parent or responsible adult could have prevented the situation from happening.

Children require a certain amount of guidance and dogs require a great deal of supervision. Unsupervised matching of the pair has, on occasion, led to disastrous results and responsible adults should always assess the nature and character of their human and canine charges along with the prevailing circumstances before giving them joint freedom.

REMEDIAL AND PREVENTIVE ACTION YOU CAN TAKE

Remedial action comes down to basic control and education of both children and dogs. Educating children to behave in a suitable manner when in the company of dogs is, I think, more difficult than training the dogs to be suitably responsive. However, a great deal hinges on the behaviour, consideration and understanding the children have for their own or other people's canine companions.

Training the dog to the requirements of Chapter Two is an excellent means of achieving the control which will help to avoid unpleasant situations, and the involvement of the family in this training can only help to create a more responsive and considerate outlook from the children.

As remedies and preventive action principally involves the education and behaviour of children rather than dogs, I leave that in the hands of responsible parents.

The understanding of canine aggressiveness towards children is no different than the situations described in Chapter Eight and it is, therefore, advisable to become fully acquainted with the contents of that chapter.

Problem 9.2 – DOGS IN CARS

My dog can get very excited when he is in the car with me. He will bark at people passing, particularly if they have a dog with them. This happens when I am driving along the road or when I have parked.

An Understanding and Probable Causes

Many dogs become excited in the car just because they are being taken out. They may know or think that at the end of the journey there is freedom to enjoy the countryside or a romp on the beach.

This excitement can be built up into near hysteria if it is allowed to develop. If the dog does not like other dogs he will also protect his property (the car) from them. People will stop and look at dogs in cars and children will tease them with the safety of a protective glass window between them. There are many reasons for dogs in cars barking.

It is unfortunate that while travelling on the road the driver is not in a position to divide his attention between driving the car and the dog's antics. A dog knows that any verbal abuse is quite meaningless while the car is in motion and to stop the car, take effective action and then drive again creates the opportunity for him to restart his unpleasant antics.

Remedial and Preventive Action You Can Take

Control training to get and keep your dog's attention as described in Chapter Two is a good foundation to gain any measure of success, although this in itself is unlikely to achieve any lasting results. However, the aid of shock treatment and basic training can have desirable results. If a passenger is available to take action, the banging of two baking tins can induce a more responsible canine attitude. A jet of clean water can have the same effect if you do not mind getting the inside of your car wet. Although the driver of the car can apply these techniques when the car is stationary it is not a practical solution when you are driving on the road.

The mugger/rape alarm can also be effective, especially if you do not have a passenger to help out. When used in an enclosed space the type of noise from such an alarm can be very effective, and eventually the very sight of the alarm can be sufficient to prevent some dogs from starting up their noise.

What a dog does not see he will not bark at is often an effective outlook. Covered side windows or a covered travelling crate can prevent the dog from seeing and objecting to passing people or dogs. Travelling crates and indoor kennels can be one and the same thing: they can have a dual purpose. It should be noted that a cover on a travelling crate in a stationary car during very hot weather could be a very dangerous practice.

Although an inner tail gate in an estate car is of no value in calming an excited dog while on the road, a cover can be placed over it and the side windows while parked. It can prove useful in controlling and putting a lead on an excitable dog before letting him out, and it has the added advantage of providing greater ventilation when the outer tail gate is open while parked during attendance at various events in hot weather.

Corrective action should always be taken at the first indication of excitement and not left until your dog is completely out of control. Quite often the situation can be anticipated and you or your passenger can be prepared with a distracting aid to attract the dog's first signs of attention away from the object of his interest.

Problem 9.3 – DOGS AND VETS

Although my vet is very understanding and capable of handling my dog, the dog is difficult to control when being examined or administered with the appropriate treatment. He has tried to bite the vet and seems to have no trust in him at all.

An Understanding and Probable Causes

It is fortunate that most vets are capable of handling the many difficult situations that they find themselves in when treating our canine companions. Anything that a dog owner can do to make diagnosis and treatment of canine ailments easier for the vet and dog is well worth the effort.

Although unfortunate encounters with other dogs in the vet's waiting room can start a chain of unpleasant events for a dog, the most distressing experiences usually occur in the consulting/treatment room. These experiences may well be due to the dog's inherent temperament or the fact that he is spoilt and out of control.

Vets do their best: they can try to reassure a dog under the various circumstances but they may well require to use a very positive approach to achieve a proper diagnosis or to administer the appropriate treatment. The dog may not like it, will certainly not connect the vet with his improved condition and will remember the unpleasantness each time he visits the surgery.

Remedial Action You Can Take

Any signs of aggressiveness from your dog towards a vet requires a full understanding of canine aggression and the contents of Chapter Eight should be fully digested. The aggression may be related to fear or undisciplined dominance. The relevant section in Chapter Eight will certainly give you the basic approach to achieving a more satisfactory canine attitude.

Unfortunately most owners do not sufficiently ensure that their dogs can be handled by themselves, never mind other people. You should be able to have your dog stand, sit or lie down to be examined; to be felt over the body and limbs; to have his teeth and ears checked; and to have the pads of all four paws checked. If you or your family cannot examine your own dog in this manner you cannot expect your dog to accept such handling from an experienced vet. Periodic grooming will also help to give the dog the experience of being handled in a controlled situation.

Training to the requirements in Chapter Two will help to achieve control, but attendance at breed or obedience classes can help by having strangers check your dog without needles, probes or thermometers being unpleasantly introduced.

You may never have your dog happy when he is going to visit the vet but you should, at least, achieve a situation whereby you can hold your dog and allow the vet full freedom to diagnose the problem and to apply the appropriate treatment.

PREVENTIVE MEASURES YOU CAN TAKE

The very first visit your puppy makes to the vet is the most important and this visit should be devoid of any unpleasantness. Avoid a crowded waiting room: either keep the puppy in the car with a friend or member of the family until it is your turn or make an appointment at a quiet time of day. The first visit can be utilised to have the puppy checked over with a further appointment for the usual injections.

Other factors mentioned under the remedies heading should be carried out as preventive measures. Control training, grooming, handling by the family and friends with the pretence of purposeful physical examination are all ingredients which help to create the character and controlled response a vet likes to see in his surgery.

Problem 9.4 – AVOIDANCE OF RECOGNISED PROBLEMS

Many problems are of such a nature that the remedies can be difficult to achieve under the situations which cause them and avoiding the situation is generally the best way to overcome them. On occasion a lengthy period of avoidance can be a cure in itself, so that when the dog is given the opportunity to restart the undesirable activity he will have matured out of the habit or other more constructive activities will be taking up his mind.

Some situations where avoidance is much simpler than trying to apply doubtful remedies have already been discussed. Sheep chasing and the chasing of motor cars or cycles are discussed in Problems 7.4 and 7.5, for example. One further avoidable situation is now discussed to highlight the importance of thinking and acting to prevent rather than to try and cure a problem.

Breaking Out of Gardens

My dog can always seem to find a way out of the garden so that he can go and play with other dogs in the neighbourhood.

An Understanding and Avoiding Action

Small dogs seem to be able to find weaknesses in the garden fence and the bigger the garden the more opportunities there are for the escape artist. Large dogs learn to jump and some garden gates or fences are no obstacle. Unfortunately, once a dog has experienced the pleasures of free ranging out of the garden it can be very difficult to keep him within the confines of the garden when he is left unsupervised.

The problem usually starts with little inquisitive puppies finding easy exits from a garden which has not been properly puppy-proofed. The desire to get out has been created by giving the puppy unsupervised freedom of the garden and boredom plus activity in the outside world has induced his first solo venture into this big world.

If your dog has been left unsupervised in the garden it must be properly fenced to prevent escape. If adequate proofing is out of the question, then unsupervised freedom must also be out of the question.

Outdoor Kennels

A kennel in a suitable corner of the garden and with a small fenced exercise area can be the answer to many problems but an unplanned introduction to such a kennel can create a great deal of canine mental stress and, therefore, introduce other problems.

The basic principles of conditioning for an indoor kennel as described in Problem 5.10 will again apply. Your dog's bed from indoors can be put into the kennel for his initial short spells of isolation. His meals can be given in the kennel or run and a short spell in his kennel after exercise when he can recharge his batteries with a sleep are ideal occasions to get your dog accustomed to spells of restricted outdoor life.

Any problem in the garden, be it escaping, digging, jumping gates, chasing children or dogs at the other side of the fence comes into the same category. If you are not there to prevent the situation from arising, it will continue.

To shout at a dog or punish him in any way is generally useless. The dog will just do it again when you disappear back into the house. It should always be your policy to avoid such situations if you have no means of controlling them.

Remember that a dog will always do what he considers to be in his best interest at that particular moment in time.

Although the avoidance of certain situations can be advisable, the training routines in Chapter Two will create a more controllable and responsive dog along with a more constructively active canine mind.